... One expert, when he was as   D0330098
ernment conference about the best strategy for ___
the homosexuality problem, capsuled his advice in these
words: "prevention, prevention, prevention." And the most
effective preventive measure of all is to raise children in a
sexually sound home.

—Peter and Barbara Wyden, *Growing Up Straight*

... The best intervention for homosexuality lies in its prevention "through the early identification and treatment of the
potential homosexual child."

—F. X. Acosta, quoted by George Rekers, *Hope for Homosexuality*

The real tragedy of homosexuality is that with a little
understanding, love and help from the parents of these victims this would not have happened at all.... It seems obvious
that if the cure for homosexuality is difficult, we should
devote our efforts to preventive action.

—David Wilkerson, *Homosexuality Begins at Home*

The early detection of sexual problems in youth permits
treatment interventions that can prevent the ... distressing
sexual disorders of adulthood ... [and] requires that the non-
specialist in sexual disorders be equipped to recognize, treat
and/or refer young patients for appropriate interventions.

—George Rekers, *Handbook of Child and Adolescent Sexual
Problems*

We view your encouragement of prevention as tantamount to genocide, and of treatment as tantamount to
recruitment of gay people into heterosexuality.

—Franklin E. Kameny, letter dated May 10, 1997 addressed
to Gary Bauer, President, Family Research Council,
Washington, D.C.

An Ounce of
Prevention

An Ounce of
Prevention

*Preventing the Homosexual Condition
in Today's Youth*

Don Schmierer
with **Lela Gilbert**

Promise Publishing Co. Santa Ana, CA 92711

ISBN 0-939497-61-1

Printed in the United States of America
00 01 02 03 04 QPV 6 5 4 3

I dedicate this book to my wife, Diana; to my parents who instilled in us Biblical truth and values; to our sons who are very supportive and did a great job of raising their parents; and to "His Servants" partners who believed in us enough to invest themselves, their prayers, and their resources in our ministry.
I thank God for all of you.

Contents

Contents

Introduction

WHAT IS OUR SOCIETY COMING TO?" In homes, churches, restaurants—anywhere people gather and talk—both secular and religious communities are asking this question. The media report horror stories involving gang warfare, road rage, random shootings, scandal among respected leaders—the list goes on and on. The overload of bad news has simply desensitized some to what is happening around them.

My research confirms that thirty years ago discussions about dealing with society's ills were prevention-oriented. What happened? If we in the Western world had stayed on the path of prevention, would we be experiencing the moral crisis we now face?

Addressing root problems is the issue, and most painful root problems manifest themselves in an array of addictive behaviors, which may also include displays of anger. Our present Western world is basically a wounded and angry society heading in a very destructive direction, a reality that is sadly confirmed by turning on the nightly news. In a world of hurt, we cannot just put our heads in the sand and hope the problem will somehow disappear. In fact, our refusal to involve ourselves in the issue only makes matters worse.

Among a constellation of other factors, the crises we face

have much to do with parenting. They also have roots in the society surrounding children and the ways it influences a young person's thinking. In this book, *An Ounce of Prevention*, I am focusing our specific attention on one issue that represents only one aspect of modern destructive patterns—that of homosexuality. I hope to challenge your thinking processes with the idea that homosexuality can indeed be prevented, even from the beginning of one's life. Prevention of homosexuality begins in the home, in the earliest years of childhood. In this book I will explore, in some depth, the multitude of issues that contribute to homosexuality, with the emphasis on prevention.

Sometimes youths of either sex are placed in environments where homosexuality can be forced on them by those in power. . . . Obviously everything should be done to prevent the occurrence of such situations. . . . These things may not prevent homosexuality in every case . . . but if, as I believe, it is a disease due to environment and upbringing, it is only common sense to give the child and youth the best possible chance to grow up normally. —Charles Berg, M.D./Clifford Allen, M.D., 1958

Diana and I enlisted the help of researchers and a writer for this book. They are all committed Christians who seek to love, obey, and serve our heavenly Father through a personal vital relationship with his Son and our Savior, the Lord Jesus Christ. Our individual and corporate desire is to "walk as Jesus did" (1 John 2:6) and to be "God's fellow workers" (1 Corinthians 3:9) in fulfilling his design and purposes for the world.

It is my conviction that we in the Christian community

must first take a long hard look at ourselves before pointing any fingers at others (1 Peter 4:17–5:4). I believe God wants to accomplish positive change through his Church. I have written this book from the perspective that we are part of the problem and need to be leaders in finding solutions. Would you not agree that if Christians would work together, with God's help, we would stand a very real chance of impacting the culture and changing the direction of society?

Diana and I wanted to get involved in the issue of homosexuality because of a discussion we had with a very close friend about AIDS hospice work and whether it could be sufficiently continued once new and stricter government regulations began to be enforced. Our friend made a very profound statement to me: "Don, you need to work on preventing these problems from happening in the first place instead of putting endless effort into 'fixing' them—you're losing ground." That statement jolted my thinking and I soon began a research journey that resulted in the writing of this book.

An Ounce of Prevention is structured in two parts. The first part is an overview, which provides the "big picture" about homosexuality, including facts that may be new to you. In the second section of the book, I share some of my personal experiences in dealing with the issue and factors to be dealt with if prevention of homosexuality is going to happen.

Diana and I are founders of a ministry known as "His Servants." We've been married for thirty-eight years and have two sons and two granddaughters. Just for the record, our sons did not have perfect parents—we made many mistakes in raising them. Our family has faced the pain of seeing both sons through the experience of divorce. Our love, respect, and relationship have been greatly enhanced through life's trials and in various Christian ministries for the past forty years.

My interest in helping and counseling young people began in discipleship ministry on five military bases while I was in the Navy in Hawaii. Our ministry experience grew through teaching youth and adult Sunday school classes and serving on boards of elders over a thirty-year span. We started and developed a university ministry and worked in marriage and family counseling, 12-step programs for addictive behaviors, youth programs, businessmen's leadership groups, and a ministry to women. Diana and I have always operated as a husband and wife team working at our agricultural profession to supply the majority of our needs.

While writing this book, I have worked closely with a friend whom we will call "Cody." Cody was once involved in the homosexual lifestyle and took an active role in the movement. He "came out" of the lifestyle and became involved in founding a pioneer AIDS hospice in the United States, developing it after the model established by Mother Teresa. He was active in starting a total of eleven hospices; Cody has buried hundreds of AIDS patients.

Cody has been a very valuable resource person and has provided a wealth of important information in helping to formulate this book. Diana and I consider him a son and a very dear brother in the Lord. Knowing him, hearing his story, and feeling the pain of his past have given us new insights and appreciation for those who have experienced rejection and abuse beginning at a very young age. We regret not being able to provide more of Cody's life struggles, giving him due credit and the exposure his efforts deserve.

Lela Gilbert is working with us as a writer. Without her abilities, experience, and awareness of the subject, Diana and

I would be nowhere. We thank the Lord for bringing her across our path. She is a dear friend, a mature sister in the Lord, and has taught and helped us immensely.

In writing this book, I am using the Bible as the final authority for my conclusions. I believe the Bible is God's Word and that it "says what it means and means what it says." Most times in life this has been very comforting to me, but it has also challenged my thinking and motivated me to redirect my life.

In his *Daily Thoughts for Disciples*, Oswald Chambers wrote, "Many people are enchanted with the gospel—but few are changed." Let's hope and pray that we are more than enchanted. My prayer is that this book impacts your life and faith to the degree that you will join me in becoming "biblical change agents" in today's troubled world. In doing so, the question "What is our society coming to?" can be answered with hope and praise: "By God's grace, we're working toward developing a strong, healthy society."

Don Schmierer,
Sacramento, California

Part One:

Fact or Fiction?

THE SUBJECT OF HOMOSEXUALITY is replete with myths, misinformation, and misunderstandings. Most of us have been exposed to a plethora of rumors, unsubstantiated opinions, and unproved theories about "gay" men and women and how they got that way. Many Christians have abstract ideas about the subject that they've never tried to apply to real situations. Others have chosen to take the "ostrich" approach—pretend the issue doesn't exist, at least not in "our church," "our school," or "our family." Still others have adopted an "I'm okay, you're okay" attitude toward most moral choices in general and this one in particular.

Meanwhile, young girls and boys all around us are struggling with deep questions about gender, intimate relationships, emotional longings, and Christian spirituality. Are we prepared to reach out to them, to love them, to affirm them, and to make it possible for them to build a deep and abiding relationship with God through Jesus Christ? Or are we in danger of turning them away because of our own fears, ignorance, and self-righteousness?

If there is one thing we have learned, it is that those who are closest to the issue of homosexuality suffer with the deepest imaginable wounds. Pain is the common denominator among countless variations and scenarios, and misunderstanding and unforgiveness can profoundly increase that pain.

Our primary purpose is to reach out loving hands toward those who are hurting. We also hope to increase the understanding of those who care about a specific young person or group of young people, those who care about healing broken hearts, and those who hope to find their own answers to some of life's toughest questions.

In the first part of our book, we want to introduce the subject of homosexuality in terms of the best information we could find. We've collected stories about real people, changing names, places, and circumstances to protect the identity of those involved. We've contrasted popular myths with documented facts, some of which come to us from the homosexual community. And we've tried to offer suggestions for those who want to make a difference in some very important young lives.

Once we've laid a foundation for understanding, we'll move on to part 2, in which we will apply the information we've learned to some specific situations.

Chapter One

What Is Homosexuality, Really?

Jason and Ryan, brothers who both attend a small, suburban high school, came home laughing about a new student named Lonny. "He's telling everybody he's gay," Jason reported to their mother. "And he definitely is," Ryan agreed. "You should see him."

"What do you mean? What does he look like?"

"He's such a girl. He's the worst athlete in the world, and he thinks he's a fashion plate. He is so gay . . ."

"So you guys think every male who's not an athlete is gay?"

"You don't understand. It's not just that. It's the way he walks and talks and dresses too. He's gay. He says so, and so does everybody else."

The mother asked whether Lonny seemed to have a "boyfriend" or whether he talked about a relationship.

"No," Jason explained. "He says he's never been with anybody yet. But his mom knows he's gay, and I guess she thinks it's fine. He hangs out with the girls, talking about clothes and hair, or he just acts like a loner."

3

"Does he have any male friends?" the mother asked.
"Are you kidding? Nobody wants to be seen with him. If we
tried to talk to him, everybody would think we were gay too."

REACTIONS LIKE THIS from teenagers like Ryan and Jason are typical. Their response to the issue of homosexuality is to escape from it as quickly as possible. All they want to know is that they aren't "like that." Their natural reaction to those whose sexual "preference" threatens their own sexual identity and feeds their own barely-submerged sexual insecurities is to cut and run.

The words *gay* and *homosexual* have become so much a part of modern vocabulary that most people rarely stop to consider their meaning. Popular usage defines *gay* as pertaining to individuals interested in "same-sex" physical relationships. When homosexuality is mentioned in the media it is often referred to as an "alternative lifestyle," though that lifestyle is as alien to many Americans as the lost continent of Atlantis.

For many teens and young adults, homosexuality evokes fear, revulsion, mockery, and various other defenses, thus distancing them from the people involved. Empathy, concern, and compassion for practicing homosexuals aren't priorities for them.

Those of us who identify with the Christian community, who are conservative, or who think of ourselves as "traditionalists," are also content to keep ourselves well removed from men and women who are involved in the "gay lifestyle."

It seems the less we know about all that, the better. The greater the distance between us, the safer we will feel. What little we have learned about their "sex acts" disgusts us, and whatever health or legal challenges they face are clearly *their* problem, not ours. But most of us, either consciously or subconsciously, are haunted by some key questions whose answers could seriously impact the way we live, raise our children, and relate to this frequently alienated group of people:

- Can homosexuality be prevented in the first place?
- Can homosexuals change their sexual behavior?
- What sets people up to be attracted to homosexuality?

It may surprise you to hear that I believe that the answer to the first two questions is clearly YES. In fact, the purpose of this book is to provide an overview of factors that contribute to the choice of a homosexual lifestyle with prevention of this choice in mind and to outline some effective preventive strategies.

What Is Our First Priority?

What do we mean when we say Christian? In Acts 11:26 we read, "The disciples were called Christians first at Antioch." A disciple is a follower, and a Christian disciple is one who follows Jesus' example of a life so full of love that he was willing to die for the sins of people who hated him to bring them to the knowledge of God. That's what I'm thinking about when I use the word Christian. That's the lifestyle people are referring to when they say to love the sinner and hate the sin.

To really feel Christ's compassion for those caught up in homosexuality, it is extremely important for us to understand

5

that great human suffering is frequently reflected in the lives of these people. There is often great pain in such people's backgrounds—pain which entails abuse and emotional abandonment resulting in a profound sense of rejection.

If a boy or girl chooses to move from same-sex attraction into the homosexual lifestyle, great losses are incurred; indentity confusion, depression, family and social exile, stormy and intense same-sex relationships, blood-borne diseases, and a greater likelihood of drug and alcohol abuses.

Secondly, and worse still, the young men and women who struggle with homosexuality are faced with heart-breaking spiritual concerns. They usually feel cut off from God, unable to reconcile their "gay" persona with Christianity or other religious systems that disapprove of homosexuality. They find themselves set adrift, and all too often they are deserted by the very people who should care the most about their circumstances—past, present, future, and eternal. As Christians we are called to love hurting and lost souls such as these (1 John 4:7–12).

Jesus taught that all behavior begins in the mind when he equated looking at another with lust with committing a sexual sin. Paul said that only with God's help are any of us "transformed by the renewing of our minds" through a process of spiritual rebirth (Romans 12:2). Because of this, we must first consider a person's spiritual status before we concern ourselves with the specifics of any sinful condition—heterosexual or homosexual.

Since you are reading this book, you are probably concerned about someone's sexual identity. Has that person been introduced to the Christ of the Gospels? Real change always begins when Christ's Spirit is free to work within us and through us. Jesus declared,

> "I tell you the truth, no one can see the kingdom of God unless he is born again . . . For God so loved the world that he gave his one and only Son, that whoever believes in him shall not perish but have eternal life. For God did not send his Son into the world to condemn the world, but to save the world through him." (John 3:3, 16–17)

Our first priority, then, is to reach out to others in Christian love, praying for opportunities to share the good news about Jesus with all who will hear. Our primary responsibility is not to condemn others or to be moral reformers. It is, rather, to joyfully communicate and demonstrate the truth about Jesus Christ's life, his death on the cross for the sins of us all, and his victory over the grave and to show others that we have a living Savior who intercedes for us day and night. No matter how we may have sinned in thought, word, or deed, when we come to him—just the way we are—he will unfailingly receive us, redeem us, remake us, and impart to us his peace. Outside of Christ's transforming power, human beings cannot change their sinful inner condition. Forcing a few external changes on people to please conventional norms will not set them free in a powerful way so they can follow Jesus' plan for their lives and experience real spiritual freedom and wholeness.

⟶

A POPULAR MYTH: Once you decide to become involved in homosexual behavior, there is no way back—you can't change your direction.
Consider this: Homosexual behaviors are

preventable and treatable in many cases. As with any other sexual sin, if we confess sinful behavior to God (1 John 1:9), he will forgive the sin and cleanse the sinner. Sometimes boys find themselves feeling emotionally attached to other boys, and the same is true of some girls. This is not the same as homosexual behavior, although it could, under certain conditions, lead to it. The sooner any tendencies toward homosexual behavior are detected, the easier it is to prevent them.

~~~~~~~

Psychologists Stanton Jones and Mark Yarhouse of Wheaton College state that eighty years of genuine research suggests strongly that homosexuality is quite changeable. They say, "Every study ever performed on conversion from homosexual to heterosexual orientation has produced . . . successes that ranged between 33 percent and . . . 60 percent." Numerous success stories are on record among the more than two hundred self-help support groups in the U.S. and elsewhere. Some of the major networks are Courage, Exodus, and Homosexuals Anonymous.

Patterns of Homosexual Development

Of course, we are faced with many challenges as we choose to play a loving role in the prevention of homosexual behavior. But before considering those challenges, let's first take a look at the process which carries a developing boy or girl from same-sex attraction into what we call the "homosexual condition" and on toward the homosexual lifestyle. By way of definition, this is what we mean:

Same-sex Attraction
is a set of deficits—physical, emotional, and environ-
mental—that set the stage for the homosexual *condition.*

Deficits

Tendencies

Attractions

The Homosexual Condition
may involve sexual acting out, experimentation, and
eventually, some level of involvement in . . .

The Homosexual Lifestyle
sometimes described as "gay" or the "gay lifestyle."

What Does *Deficits* Mean?

The chart above mentions "deficits" which set the stage for
the homosexual condition. These deficits many have manifested very early in a child's life. Other problems, especially
those involving abuse, may even begin in infancy. Many of
the physical problems that lead to social ostracism become
apparent in elementary school, long before puberty. These
physical problems may include a chronic illness, a handicap,
or a hormonal deficiency. In a boy, it could be as simple as
nearsightedness, combined with a lack of athletic coordination
or skill. These may well cause him to be an outcast when
teams are chosen for sports or a subject of ridicule when an
athletic competition requires his participation. Some studies

have indicated that a lack of athletic ability alone accounts for the sexual identity confusion faced by many males. But of course there are gay athletes, and all heterosexual boys don't have athletic interests.

> *Peers are merciless in persecuting anyone they even suspect of homosexuality. A boy who shies away from competitive sports may be exposed to his peers in the same way as a girl who is too aggressive—each becomes targeted. —Gershen Kaufman1*

A girl's struggles with sexuality may begin when she is considered "unattractive" by her classmates. She may struggle with a weight problem, or she may not have natural "style" or "beauty." In both boys and girls, physical challenges might involve a hearing or speech impediment, crippling disorders, learning disabilities, deformities, or unsightly skin conditions.

These deficits may set the stage for homosexual tendencies when physical limitations are accompanied by heightened emotional sensitivity, triggering peer rejection, unpopularity, isolation, and labeling as a "geek," a "loser," or some other popular epithet. In short, the child is excluded from the larger social group. Even worse, the child may not measure up to the parents' expectations, resulting in disapproval or withdrawal on the part of the parents, whose lack of affirmation can be wounding to the child.

Of course, the likelihood of gender confusion is greatly exaggerated if there is a hormonal imbalance involved—this is typically demonstrated when boys are chemically inclined to appear to be unusually feminine or when girls seem unduly masculine. Hormonal imbalances are medically treatable, but parents and other concerned adults often overlook them. Imbalances can also be treated unwisely, causing even more complications. Along with an array of other problems, the mannerisms, appearance, and behaviors related to hormonal imbalances usually generate teasing, mocking, and harassment. Meanwhile, during a child's early development when identity confusion occurs in all children, boys may mimic female behaviors and mannerisms, and girls, male.[2] The inevitable social rejection creates insecurities, which, in turn, hinder comfortable and healthy friendships.

Lonny had been a sickly toddler, and by the time he reached first grade, he was highly dependent on asthma medication. He often missed weeks of school during the spring and fall allergy seasons. But the biggest challenge to Lonny was neither his small size nor his constant wheezing. It was his inability or unwillingness to participate in outdoor games, either during recess, in physical education classes, or with the children in his neighborhood.

Lonny adamantly refused to play baseball, football, kickball, or even informal games of tag and hide-and-seek. This was the case even on days when his asthma was under control. Throughout his elementary school years, he usually retreated to the sidelines and ended up with a group of girls. He was more than happy to play house with them while the other boys competed in physically demanding activities.

Obviously, some children are more socially successful than others, and children are generally cruel to their peers. However, any child who is continuously rejected by same-sex peers develops a chronic sense of being an outsider, a misfit, a pariah. And this low image of self may cause him or her to conclude, "I'm different. Something is wrong with me. I'm not normal." When this is the case, consolation and companionship from friends of the opposite sex may actually do more to incite gender confusion than to resolve it.

Of course, many children who face these difficulties can thrive *if* they have supportive parents or the help of other concerned adults. In fact, social struggles can encourage some children to become exceptional in other areas. But all too often, because of complex family issues, the socially unaccepted children who most need support at home simply don't get it.

How Does Home Life Make a Difference?

Physical challenges take their toll on all kids, and most boys and girls go through periods of social struggle. But the length and impact of these episodes is dramatically compounded when a child's family situation is less than ideal. Good parenting is a key factor in the raising of healthy children. Conversely, a lack of good parenting—most notably good fathering—is a major contributor to the homosexual condition. Nearly all studies dealing with homosexuality— both pro and con—reflect a pattern of father/child relationships that is both unhealthy and unhappy. Dad is a key player in the sexual identity game.

Children who develop homosexual tendencies often have fathers who are absent. If they are present in the home, they may be emotionally absent, meaning they are either wrapped up in their own world, drunk, or addicted to drugs, always on the phone or computer, or they are simply emotionally inept or otherwise unreachable by their children.

Mothers also play an important role in the formation of their children's sexual identity. When examining the parental patterns underlying the homosexual condition, we find that mothers of sexually confused children are often domineering and excessively critical and/or controlling. They may be women who have learned to hate men and therefore demean all males. They may be lonely, needy single women who develop emotionally incestuous relationships with their sons. They may be women who seek to control everyone—males and females alike—simply because of their own fear, anger, and frustration.

Lonny's parents were never close, and his father was often absent from the home. His mother, a highly emotional woman of great artistic talent, became intensely protective of her sickly son. Sparked by disappointment and fear, she poured all her emotional energy into her only child. As Lonny grew, she became more and more emotionally dependent on him. His needs became her needs; his problems became the center of her life.

Lonny's isolation from his father and his peers drove him further into his mother's protective embrace. His feelings for her and for his father were confused and ambivalent. He longed for his father's attention, but he hated him for his lack of paternal interest and for his inability to defend himself against his wife's incessant criticism. Meanwhile, as Lonny approached adolescence, his mother's controlling personality and her emotional outbursts infuriated him, while at the same time a deep bond linked him to her. In some ways, he felt like an extension of her life—her talents, her tantrums, and her troubles.

It is not unusual to find that boys who have chosen a homosexual lifestyle are the youngest in the family, the only child, or have been adopted.[3] Another source of problems may be that the parents wanted a child of the opposite gender;

they may have unconsciously cultivated characteristics of the desired gender in their child, causing the child to be confused about his or her gender. Those same parents may even communicate, "You were an unwanted child."

These examples are certainly not true for all cases—I will later examine the warning signs of children who are at risk, and we will quickly see that there are no absolutes. However, there are some common denominators. And one of the most common, and the most tragic, is sexual abuse.

It is not difficult to imagine why sexual molestation contributes to confusion about sexual identity. A boy who has been molested by another male may come to believe that he was "born" to engage in same-sex behavior. A girl, whose father or some other adult male has repeatedly abused her, may determine that she will never in her life freely give herself sexually to another male. She may feel safe only with females.

⤝⤞

A POPULAR MYTH: Homosexual behavior has nothing to do with sexual abuse

Consider this: Sexual abuse is a key factor in homosexuality. Studies indicate that as many as 58 percent of homosexuals have experienced sexual abuse as children; many of the rest were physically or emotionally abused.[4]

⤝⤞

Can the Home Environment Lead to Homosexuality?

Certainly caring parents hope to shield their children from the horrors of abuse. But exactly what kind of environment fosters healthy sexual development of children? The ideal and worthy goal of most concerned parents, whether single or married is an environment with frequent affection, positive role modeling, and wholesome entertainment.

But some kids spend their developmental years in circumstances where arguing, fighting, or icy estrangement between parents provides no clear idea about how healthy men and women should relate to one another. These children learn hate, not love. To make matters worse, their unhappy parents sometimes pit their children against the opposing spouse, twisting loyalties and creating intense emotional bewilderment.

Other children live in homes where physical, emotional, or sexual abuse is common. Affection in such homes may be nonexistent, or when it is given, affection may be inappropriate and include sexual innuendo, incest, molestation, or even rape.

Frighteningly, countless homes are polluted with pornography. This may involve "soft porn," such as popular male magazines, "girlie" photos, and sexually indiscriminate movies and videos. Or it may include graphic photography, films and publications illustrating various perversions, including sadomasochism, pedophilia, or same-sex erotica.

Children who are molested may actually be shown pornography and asked to duplicate the acts which are depicted. They may come to believe, early on, that pornography is part of "normal" adult life. They may even become addicted to pornography themselves. Pornography can heighten sexual arousal, leading to premarital and extramarital sex, and along with an assortment of other circumstances, the presence of pornography creates the backdrop—the tendencies—against which same-sex attractions may take place.

During her husband's frequent travels, Lonny's mother befriended a handsome young artist who was attracted to her and to her work. Blinded by her infatuation, she allowed him to live in their house for a few months. During his stay with them, and unbeknownst to Lonny's mom, he sexually molested the little boy several times.

Lonny, although less than five years old, was left with fairly vivid memories of the sexual encounters. The man, who was always sketching Lonny as the subject of various art projects, drew the boy and himself in pornographic poses—poses which he actually acted out with Lonny. These incidents were not unpleasant to Lonny, and he never told his mother about them. Craving fatherly attention and unaware of the perversion involved, for the first time, Lonny felt loved. When the molester moved out, Lonny was sad and assumed that yet another male had abandoned him. It was because of this relationship with his mother's lover that Lonny said, as a teenager, "I've always been gay—as long as I can remember I've wanted to be with boys, not girls."

How Do Tendencies Become Attractions?

Do all kids with deficits or physical handicaps become homosexual? No.

Do all children from unhappy homes choose the homosexual lifestyle? No.

Do all girls and boys who are from unhealthy home environments have problems with gender identity? No.

Although these three areas are critical, we will see in the chapters that follow that there are an infinite number of variables involved in the development of same-sex attraction. And same-sex attraction doesn't always become a homosexual condition.

16

Children whose lives have been marred by unhealthy circumstances may become confused about their feelings for others of the same sex. Innocent emotional attractions toward others that spring from a normal need for appropriate affection and relationships with those of the same sex may be misunderstood by these children or those around them. Unless some form of healthy intervention takes place, they may become trapped in tendencies that lead to homosexual acting out.

"Gay" Sex: Experiment or Lifetime Condition?

For a long time Lonny had fantasized about sexual acts, and in recent years, he had used homosexual pornography while masturbating. At a class party, where alcohol and drugs flowed freely, Lonny found himself sexually involved with a very intoxicated male student named Justin. The two boys participated in a sex act, and several other students found out about it. Rumors energized the phone lines all weekend, and by Monday morning, both boys had been labeled "gay" by their fellow students.

Are Lonny and Justin, in fact, gay?

The answer is no. Although they have participated in a homosexual act, they are not necessarily homosexual. Lonny is following a pattern moving from same-sex attractions into a full-fledged homosexual condition. The other boy did a regrettable thing while under the influence of drugs and alcohol in an isolated incident. Such an encounter would have been just as regrettable had he done something of a similar nature with a girl. In any case, the act the two boys engaged in does not indicate with finality that either of them is a homosexual.

The boys should not be labeled homosexual because,

first, *no one really is homosexual in essence.* There are certainly people who participate in homosexual acts and who identify with the homosexual community. But they are, in reality, simply men and women who have chosen or are choosing a certain type of behavior. Their inner being, their spirit and soul, cannot be defined as a homosexual entity.

Second, adolescent sexual experimentation may include homosexual acts. This can be the result of curiosity, of lust, of the inability to find an opposite-sex partner, or of angry rebellion and a desire to act in ways that provide guaranteed shock value.

> The homosexual condition is a deviation from healthy sexuality. It needn't be considered a permanent state of being. It is not a third gender. It is not a lifestyle destiny, sealed by some mysterious fate. It is a condition, one which can be changed, altered, and—when wisely recognized at an early stage—prevented.

Unfortunately, when the warning signs remain unrecognized, are ignored, or are responded to with rejection, same-sex attraction can result in sexual acting out. And that sexual acting out can spin out of control into a downhill spiral—entry into the homosexual lifestyle.

Why Prevention?

There is an old saying, "An ounce of prevention is worth a pound of cure." When the risks involved in the homosexual lifestyle are honestly weighed, far more than a pound of cure is necessary to save the lives of those involved. In fact, in at least half the cases, the tragic consequences of the homosexual lifestyle may be virtually incurable.

On the other hand, there are many reasons to believe that same-sex attraction and the homosexual condition can and should be prevented and, as with many problems in society, this one begins in the home.[5] In chapter 5 we will consider some of the risks and reasons for concern that are clearly evident in homosexual behavior and the homosexual lifestyle. But for now, let's focus on the world's way of looking at homosexuality.

In our present culture, it is considered "politically incorrect" to say that homosexual behavior is a form of sexual perversion. In fact, the popular media would have us believe that there is no such thing as sexual perversion; only the most violent, bizarre, and macabre acts qualify as such. Other less dramatic sex acts—whomever and whatever they involve—fall under the popular umbrella of "different strokes for different folks." However, it hasn't always been this way.

As early as 1933, prevention was considered to be the best option in dealing with the issue of homosexuality and, even then, prevention strategy was directed at the family environment. Dr. William Stekel wrote, "I can state from my own professional experience that the parents of homosexuals always show abnormal character traits. With remarkable frequency male homosexuals have mothers who are . . . the emotional, domineering type of woman . . . just as frequently, a pathologic father, a home tyrant . . . Careful investigation of life histories will make the subject plain."[6]

Only since 1973 has homosexuality been widely viewed as a "lifestyle alternative," instead of a form of sexual deviation. This change of definition took place when the American Psychiatric Association deleted homosexuality from their *Diagnostic and Statistical Manual* as a psychological disorder. The APA was pressured by homosexual political activists to redefine the term in their publications. Even the word "gay," which implies joy, lightheartedness, and good health, was inappropriately applied to a way of life that rarely proves itself to be joyful, lighthearted, or healthy.

In his book *Homosexuality and the Politics of Truth*, Jeffrey Satinover writes, "The APA vote to normalize homosexuality was driven by politics, not science."[7] There were no clinical, scientific arguments to justify the change in assessment. The pressure was applied on the association by militant homosexual activists who, through threats of disruption and disorder, accused the psychiatrists of discrimination, not of scientific inaccuracy. In fact, five years later, a poll of 2,500 American members of the APA reported that 68 percent of them still considered homosexuality to be a psychological disorder.

It was at about this same time when the preventative approach to the homosexual condition, long a staple of the psychological and medical communities, decreased in both discussion and emphasis.[8] Because of the activism of an angry and aggressive "gay-rights" political lobby, the appeal to look upon homosexuality as a civil rights issue, and the resultant media disinformation, a preventative approach to homosexuality was virtually discontinued in most therapy environments.

Many of those who have spent years researching this subject have continued to believe that the homosexual condition is, in fact, a psychological disorder. People of faith also see it as a condition of sin and, as such, it bears a striking resemblance to numerous patterns of addictive and obsessive-compulsive behavior. Other forms of psychological dysfunction and disorder are widely treated through various forms of therapy and spiritual counseling. Why not this one?

The proclivities that lead to various high-risk behaviors—alcohol and drug abuse, anorexia and bulimia, sexual addictions and aberrations—can be identified early and addressed before their self-destructive habit patterns have severely marred or destroyed the lives of those at risk. The same is clearly true of same-sex attraction. The sooner it is identified and addressed, the more likely a preventative approach is to be successful.

Why address this issue in such a way? In recent decades, our Western world has been attempting to turn the tide against smoking because tobacco smoke, both active and passive, is dangerous. When using automobiles, we have forced our children and ourselves to wear seatbelts, because seatbelts save lives. We have actively and continually fought to save our younger generations from drug abuse, because of the outrageous risks involved.

A clear, honest look at homosexual behavior and the homosexual lifestyle provides us with ample reason for concern and for action. Prevention is not only possible, it is expedient. For those who know and understand the facts, the prevention of homosexuality is far from discrimination. It is, above all else, an act of love.

My brothers, if one of you should wander from the truth and someone should bring him back, remember this: Whoever turns a sinner from the error of his way will save him from death and cover over a multitude of sins. (James 5:19)

A New Beginning

Lonny was called into the school counselor's office. He was asked about his rumored statements regarding homosexual behavior. Later that week, his mother was also called in and informed about her son's "chosen" identity. For a few moments she sat in stunned silence.

When the therapist asked her what she was thinking, she looked at Lonny with concern, "I'll always love him no matter what he does, but a lot of my gay friends have died of AIDS, and a couple of them who didn't even have AIDS have committed suicide. I guess if it really is a choice, I'd like to try to help Lonny decide to go in a different direction."

"What about you, Lonny?" the counselor asked the boy. "What would you like to do?"

Lonny, as always, wanted to please his mother. But he was confused. "You're born gay, aren't you?" he asked, his voice puzzled. "Like, I've always been this way. I don't think I have a choice!"

The counselor shook his head, "Maybe you haven't always been this way. Maybe there are some things that changed your mind along the way . . . things that happened a long time ago . . ."

A Christian friend referred Lonny and his mother to a counselor who specialized in the prevention of homosexuality. It was his view that such a treatment is both wise and possible. The process hasn't been easy, but the fact that Lonny had only had one homosexual encounter, apart from his early molestation, has simplified matters considerably.

Today, there is good cause to believe that Lonny will choose a heterosexual lifestyle. There are many reasons for encouraging him to do so. And there is great hope that, because of his willingness, his counselor's Christian commitment, and his mother's loving concern, the process will be completed. With God's help, it will be successful.

Signs That an Adolescent May Be Struggling with Gender Issues
None of these are clear-cut indications of homosexual tendencies. However, if several of them are evident, the young person may be struggling with gender issues.

1. A sensitive child being forced to feel different because of mocking or downgrading by peers or family
2. A young boy who hangs out with girls exclusively; history of playing with girls instead of boys prior to puberty
3. Effeminate behavior/appearance in boys or extreme macho behavior; mannish style and "butch" posturing in girls (not to be confused with simply being athletic)
4. Unnatural friendship that is compulsive, secretive, or inseparable developing between siblings, cousins, relatives, or neighbors—especially in merged families or foster families
5. Exaggerated rejection by same sex parent
6. Fatherless home or emotionally unavailable father
7. Dominant mother
8. Youngest male child
9. Young girls with much older female "best friend" in a relationship that excludes others of the girl's own age
10. Anger—often manifested in sarcasm, cynicism, or withdrawal
11. Frail, deformed, deaf, or otherwise "outcast"; physical appearance not socially acceptable; "slow"
12. Comments, "I must be gay," or "I guess I'm bisexual."
13. Loner, preoccupied with self
14. Boys may avoid fights/physical altercations

Chapter Two

In Search of
"The Perfect Family"

Chad sat in the bleachers, his baseball cap turned backward, his elbows on his knees, idly watching the basketball team warm up. Just as the game was about to begin, the Sanders family came into the gym, and Chad felt the familiar inner stirring their presence always seemed to inspire. Sure, he kind of liked Sarah. But that wasn't it. They were a beautiful family, tall, attractive, and outgoing.

Tom Sanders was a highly-respected attorney in the community. His perfectly-dressed wife, Christine, was a familiar figure at the school—always involved in parent/teacher activities. And yes, Sarah, their seventeen-year-old daughter, was a knockout blonde, a cheerleader who made Chad wish he were a senior instead of a lowly sophomore. Of course the reason they were at the game was their son, Brian, an all-star basketball player who, as a junior, had already broken all the school records for points per game, steals, and rebounds.

Chad was never sure that his reaction to the Sanders was only because of the small crush on Sarah that he cherished and carefully hid from his friends. More likely, he figured, it was his own sorry home life that made him long to be part of such a model family. Chad could not imagine an occasion of any kind that would attract either of his divorced parents to the school: sports, scholastic awards, plays, homecoming—nothing interested them in the least. Chad had played baseball for years and never once had his father appeared in the crowd to cheer him on. His mom showed up only to drive him home, and then she sat in the car and listened to the radio until the game was over. She didn't know a home run from a home furnishings sale at the mall.

Chad watched the Sanders greeting all the other parents, waving cheerfully, smiling warmly, and looking for all the world like movie stars as they made their way to their seats. Just as they sat down, Tom turned around and blew a kiss at Sarah (who was looking gorgeous as ever). She smiled at him and waved, looking a little embarrassed and shy.

She shouldn't be embarrassed, Chad thought to himself. I wonder if she knows how lucky she is to have such a wonderful family. I wish my family was like that. I'd be so proud of them . . .

PERHAPS, DEEP INSIDE, every one is in search of the *Father Knows Best* family. Who wouldn't want to grow up in a beautiful suburban home, surrounded by a white picket fence, inhabited by the likes of Ward and June Cleaver or Ozzie and Harriet Nelson and their witty, trouble-free offspring? Even if we're too old to grow up there, it would be nice to live next door to these people or to ask for their wise advice when we need it. But do those kinds of families exist?

Maybe so—but we never seem to find them living on our street, in our own neighborhood, or written up in our local newspaper.

God's Perfect Family

No matter what Chad thought about the Sanders, perfect families are few and far between. In fact, when you get to know people, what you are likely to learn is a far different story. Spend any time with adolescents, and before long you'll hear some fairly serious complaints about Mom and Dad. The teenage years are hard on everybody, and the strain on even the strongest family ties is powerful and painful. Talk to parents, and you'll find that they have countless reasons to disapprove of their kids. And those same kids are equally annoyed by their parents. Even in the best of circumstances, there are misunderstandings and arguments. And in the worst of times, young people may turn to drugs, alcohol, reckless behavior, sexual acting out, or some other form of rebellion to express their anger.

Despite our white-picket-fence fantasies, most everybody knows that there's really no such thing as a perfect family. But there is a perfect plan for one. God designed the married couple to be co-creators with him, bringing new life into the world and acting as stewards of the creation. His portrait of an ideal family begins with a husband who loves and treasures his wife the way Jesus loves his Church—enough to die for her (Ephesians 5:25).

Wives are to love their husbands and to respect them as God's chosen leader of the home (Titus 2:4; Ephesians 5:33).

Children are intended to be respectful of their parents, disciplined according to their particular personalities, and not driven to exasperation by their fathers (Ephesians 6:1–2; Proverbs 22:6; Proverbs 23:13).

> So God created humankind in his image, in the image of
> God he created them; male and female he created them. God
> blessed them, and God said to them, "Be fruitful and
> multiply, and fill the earth and subdue it; and have
> dominion over the fish of the sea and over the birds of the
> air and over every living thing that moves upon the earth."
> (Genesis 1:27–28, NRSV)

It all sounds wonderful, doesn't it? God's biblical blueprint is a glorious vision for those who believe in such things, and it can become a raging hunger for those who must settle for less. To women whose husbands are rude, arrogant, or abusive, the thought of a Christlike, tenderhearted husband brings tears to the eyes. To the man whose wife is cold, distant, or angry, a loving or diligent wife (Proverbs 31) really does sound like a treasure. And to kids like Chad, involved and interested parents are, by and large, the loveliest and most impossible of dreams.

Those of us who are Christian people know that God's ideals aren't out of reach. We never quite get every detail right, but as we cooperate with his transformation of our lives, we become more and more like him, and therefore more like the kind of family members he intends for us to be. Families that use God's Word as a template for their family design come closer than most others to avoiding the pop-psych label "dysfunctional" that has become such a cliché in our modern world. When we fail, we Christians should be learning (sometimes learning the hard way) how to repent, how to forgive each other, and how to start over (1 John 1:9).

The family is God's mini-church, his sacred setting for procreation, and the most honorable of all human relationships. The family itself must be given priority as such. Each parent's role should be measured against the standards established in Holy Scripture. And the environment of the home, from before the conception of each child until the children have moved out into their own adult lives, should be God-centered, Christ-conscious, and permeated with unconditional acceptance, continuous forgiveness, encouragement, and peace. If a young couple is beginning a family, of course, the first decision to make, even before the children are born, is to bring them up in a godly way.

Christian parents are responsible to avoid the dangerous and, at times, very tempting cultural traps involving consumerism, sexual unfaithfulness, religious legalism and control, self-absorption, and uncontrolled emotions. The principles of godly parenting, which are so widely available in Christian circles, are vital to the spiritual, emotional, and even physical health of the children. And, above all else, love is the beginning, the center, and the final word to successful parenting.

Only be careful, and watch yourselves closely so that you do not forget the things your eyes have seen or let them slip from your heart as long as you live. Teach them to your children and to their children after them. (Deuteronomy 4:9)

Our Not-So-Perfect Reality

Just as Diana and I would be the first to admit that there are no perfect families, most of us know that there are no perfect people. We all do things wrong and suffer the consequences.

It has been our observation that even when we do our best, bad things can happen—death, disease, and divorce do their tragic work even in the lives of the most prayerful and faithful people. The residue of these tragedies may produce a single parent—one who never imagined being alone—trying to do the work of two parents. It may mean that children are neglected because Mom or Dad simply has to spend far too many hours every day simply trying to provide shelter, food, and clothing. Many single parents truly love their children, try their best to stay in the picture, but simply can't make it all work out the way they'd like.

Furthermore, all troubled families aren't single-parent homes. Sometimes families remain intact. There is no divorce, at least formally. But there are huge distances between the family members. Alcoholism, drug abuse, and workaholism are relentless enemies to family life. One parent may be truly committed to Christ; the other committed to his or her own agenda. No matter how devoutly they name the name of Christ, their behavior may tell a different tale.

Perhaps the lowest common denominator in all family problems is selfishness. A father may be completely wrapped up in his career, his golf, his club, his television, or his computer. A mother's devotion to her gym, her friends, her shopping, her decorating, or yes, even her church or Christian involvement can estrange her from the rest of her family. Selfishness on the part of children is not unusual. It seems to be a rather natural part of childhood, but when left unbridled, it can cause ugly tantrums, constant tension, and repetitive acts of manipulation.

We've already mentioned the terrible circumstances that persist in some families involving emotional, physical, and sexual abuse. These abuses are usually carefully hidden and may not be revealed until their damage begins to reveal itself in shocking and unexpected behaviors.

Chad could hardly believe his ears when he heard the rumor—"Sarah Sanders says she's a lesbian!" People had been talking about it all day. Someone had seen Sarah and another senior girl holding hands in the parking lot, and when they confronted her she had looked them straight in the eyes, laughed, and announced, "Yeah. So I'm a lesbian. I'll never let a man touch me. So what? Is that a problem for you?"

Chad wanted to ask her about it himself, but he didn't know her that well, and she might think he was making fun of her. So, he prudently kept his questions to himself. When he got home later that afternoon, his mother's friend Kate was at the house. "Your Mom's going to be late, so I said I'd come by and see how you're doing."

Chad liked Kate—she was loud and funny and seemed to actually be interested in him. She somehow made an effort to be around for him without being an official "baby-sitter." Since it was on his mind, he told Kate about Sarah. He didn't admit that he secretly kind of liked her (although Kate probably guessed as much), but he explained about her perfect family and the latest rumors.

"So does Sarah have a problem with boys getting too friendly?" Kate smiled. "Is she just trying to keep all you potential lover-boys away? Does she have a boyfriend?"

Chad blushed and smiled. "No way. She told me once that her father says he would be jealous if she had a boyfriend. So she doesn't go out with boys."

Kate listened carefully, and for a minute, it looked like she had tears in her eyes. "What's her father like, Chad? Does he drink?"

Chad laughed, "Are you kidding? He's the most respectable

lawyer in town. And you can tell that he really loves Sarah. He always whispers things to her and he's really affectionate—more than any other Dad I've ever seen."

Kate stared out the window for a moment, trying to decide what to say and what not to say. Finally she just shrugged and said, "Things aren't always the way they seem, Chad. That family may not be as perfect as you think it is."

Hidden Abscesses

Strange things happen behind closed doors. And they are always shocking to those who believe in the lovely façade a family constructs to camouflage its secrets. It is possible that family members themselves may not realize what is going on in a separate part of the house. A boy may be molesting his sister and may be threatening her—if she tells her parents, he'll make sure she pays dearly for it. A father may sneak into his daughter's room, perhaps when he's been drinking, and continue a secret relationship with her that she's afraid to tell anyone about—especially her mother. A man's pornography habit may be hidden at his place of work or stashed in the garage. A mother's drinking addiction may be locked away in a remote corner of the kitchen.

My life has always had silences; deep dark family secrets hidden in the attic. Secrets like incest, addiction, abuse and suicide. Growing up I found a whole different set of secrets that were my very own that stayed locked, not in the attic, but in my private closet.
—Mardi Richmond in From Wedded Wife to Lesbian Life[1]

Secrets have a way of festering in the darkness like wounds that cannot heal for lack of sunlight and air.

Christians know that Jesus called himself the light of the world and called upon his followers to be lights in the darkness around them. Of course, our own secrets must be confessed to God, and we are responsible for getting the help we need to repent and resolve them.

This is important for many reasons. First, we are all answerable to God, and we know he will hold us accountable for our sins and shortcomings. But our wrongful behavior can also have a devastating impact on those closest to us. Families that hide ugly secrets produce troubled, angry children. Sometimes those secrets aren't as dramatic as incest, molestation, and other forms of abuse. Sometimes they have to do with unhealthy emotions. With uncontrolled rage. Or untreated depression. Or relentless criticism. Parental emotional sickness is often at the root of self-destructive or addictive behavior in children.

When Sarah drove the car off the road and flipped it into the ditch, she was high on crystal meth and didn't really know what she was doing. But once she woke up in the hospital, surprisingly intact considering what could have happened to her, she began to think about the scene that had taken place at home a few weeks before. Her mother, who always started drinking at lunch, had been more drunk than usual when she'd confronted Sarah's father about his behavior towards his daughter. "You're a pervert!" she had screamed at him again and again. "You're a pedophile and a pervert. How can you look in the mirror? How can you live with yourself?"

Up until that moment, Sarah hadn't realized that her mother knew about her father's forays into her room late at night. He'd been coming to her for three years, and she had learned to hate the sound of his voice and the touch of his hands more than she could possibly say. But she was afraid—terribly afraid—of what would happen if anyone found out. First of all, when she was younger, she had kind of enjoyed the closeness she felt to him during his visits, and now that made her unbearably ashamed. Second, she knew how respected he was at the school and in the community. If anyone knew what he was really like, it would destroy his career and their wealthy lifestyle would be gone forever. Obviously, it was all her fault—she should never have let it happen in the first place.

Sarah was tortured by guilt and self-condemnation. And doing drugs made Sarah feel free—for a few hours her depression was gone; she loved the excitement of the rush. It made her actually feel happy—at least for a while. While it lasted, she was completely unconcerned about anything but good feelings and laughing hysterically with her friends. Occasionally somebody tried to get close to her sexually, but the truth was that Sarah really didn't like sex at all—with males or females. She felt filthy whenever sexual feelings arose in her, and if she followed her feelings, she found herself showering for hours on end, unable to wash away the shame and disgust that filled her soul.

Once her drug test following the accident indicated that she was using illegal substances, a court-assigned counselor began to work with her. It was several weeks before the whole story of her family life was revealed. Even then, it was only a small step toward her healing. She had so much to say, so much to face, so much to change, and so much to work through that she thought death might be easier than life.

Fortunately, her counselor believed in the spiritual principles of repentance, forgiveness, and Christian atonement. And some people Sarah hardly knew were praying for her. One of them was Chad.

Families, as God intended them to be, are the most vital, life-preserving, healthy units on earth. They are places of safety, havens from the troubles of the outside world, environments where love is given top priority. In healthy families, growth is encouraged, and children are prepared from the cradle to become strong, godly adults—ready, willing, and able to follow the calling of God. Perhaps it is for this reason that so many things can go wrong with families. In our present world, it seems as if the enemy of God uses them for target practice. There are those who actually want to ban families from existence.

> "... The family unit—spawning ground of lies, betrayals, mediocrity, hypocrisy and violence, will be abolished. The family unit, which only dampens imagination and curbs free will, must be eliminated."
> — Michael Swift, Political Radical[2]

It is precisely because of the family's key position in the world that it needs our attention, our prayers, and our commitment.

Often same-sex attraction is the product of families that have been less than perfect in areas that specifically contribute to confused sexual identity.[3] As we mentioned before, when Mom and Dad wanted Joe, Jr. to be born and Josie arrived instead, a certain amount of role confusion is caused, especially when Dad tries to turn Josie into a major league baseball player.

It also bears repeating that molestation is, in many ways, the worst offense of all. It is a deadly game. Young women like Sarah sometimes are drawn toward a homosexual condition, or even a quasi-homosexual identity (meaning that they have no intention of participating in homosexual behavior), simply to protect themselves from what they perceive as an intolerable threat of further intimacy with males. Young men who have been molested sometimes develop a homosexual condition because they have learned to function sexually in that way through molestation.

Chad talked to Kate after the news of Sarah's accident reached the school. Rumors were flying again—it wasn't long after the accident that Tom Sanders was arrested for child molestation. Because of his importance in town, it was a front-page news story.

Kate shook her head sadly. "I wish I could say I'm surprised. But I knew when you told me—deep inside I knew it all along."

"How could you possibly know that? Are you psychic or something?"

Kate smiled at her intense young friend. "No, Chad, I'm no psychic. If anything, the Lord's given me some pretty good insights. But the real reason I knew is because something like that happened to me when I was a young girl. And I've had to do a lot of work to get through the damage that was done."

"You mean you're a . . . lesbian? I thought you were married!"

Kate laughed out loud in spite of herself. "Chad, you know I'm married, and no, I never became a lesbian. But when I was young, I was very promiscuous with boys and later with more men than I could count. If I hadn't come to know the Lord, I never would have survived. Believe me, Chad. When I became a Christian, I was 'saved' in more ways than one."

"Do you hate your father? I would. That's so disgusting!"

"I did for a long time. But the Lord taught me to forgive

him. And that's not to say that what he did was right or that I decided to overlook his sick behavior. I simply had to forgive him and leave the rest with God. But a wonderful thing happened. Once I did that, it made it possible for me to actually learn to love some of the good things about him."

"Did he ever apologize?"

"No. And I never confronted him before his death. But I went to God with the past and asked God to help me get healing. And with some good counseling and my own determination to be healthy, I'm now happily married, and I love my husband very much."

Chad sighed. "I wish I didn't have so much to learn. I don't even want to know some of this stuff . . ."

"I'm sorry if I told you too much, but . . ."

"No, that's not what I meant. I'm glad you told me—really glad. I just feel so bad about the Sanders family. I really admired them. I used to wish I were in that family. Sometimes . . . I feel like I hate my parents because they ignore me and treat me like I'm invisible. But, come to think of it, maybe that's not so bad."

Kate looked at the boy with more understanding than she felt. She didn't dare tell him how negligent she thought his mother was or what a flake she thought his dad had become. Instead, she simply suggested, "Chad, I think you and I should pray for Sarah and her brother. We should ask God to lead them to forgiveness and healing. And while we're at it, let's pray for your parents too. Maybe God needs to remind them of what a great kid you are. Do you want to do that? I'll pray with you right now if you want to."

The Ripple Effect

Those of us who have been involved in decades of church work and counseling have met innumerable kids like Chad—

young men and women whose parents simply aren't interested in them. Some of them are reasonably healthy youngsters who have somehow survived their emotional abandonment. Others are involved in various kinds of trouble. We met the girls like Sarah too and their male counterparts. These are the sexual abuse victims whose lives are scarred forever by the sins of others.

We have also met a wide array of other family victims. We've heard about and sometimes seen the young people who skillfully hide bruises and welts from their repeated beatings. We've met the ones whose parents live in such an alcoholic fog that no one knows just how they manage to pay their rent and drive their cars, much less provide even a modicum of parenting. We work with the girls and boys who have lost one or both parents to jail, to cancer, to adultery, and to AIDS. We've tried to help the lost kids who've never had any real parenting at all.

The healing of family wounds—those done to families and those done by families—begins with each one of us. It extends, with its ripple effect, to the next tier: our own sons and daughters and our own parents. It moves beyond that to those of our friends and acquaintances who will benefit from our love and commitment. From there the ripples move outward toward the youth groups and counseling opportunities we have. Finally, our concern can ripple into the greater world if we choose to extend our sphere of influence. With so much trouble around us, are we discouraged? No, we aren't. We are deeply saddened, but we know that there are solutions, and we are convinced that God is able to transform even the most hopeless case into an example of his love and grace.

All this is from God, who . . . gave us the ministry of reconciliation: that God was reconciling the world to himself in Christ, not counting men's sins against them.
(2 Corinthians 5:18–20)

Where do the ripples come from? The pebble we first drop is our decision to ask God to forgive our sins toward our parents, our children, and ourselves. Then, in turn, we choose to forgive those who have wounded us. For days, months, or even years, we may have refused to look at certain aspects of our lives. We may have hidden resentments toward our parents. We may have unfinished business with our children. Before God, we must start the work with ourselves. God is faithful to point out to us the blind spots we may have missed. James 1:5 promises that if we will ask God for wisdom, he will give it freely and without reprimand. Our job is simply to receive that wisdom and to put it to work.

One of the key principles in the Christian life is forgiveness, which will be discussed in depth in chapter 9. For now, suffice it to say that forgiveness is the necessary medicine for sick and shattered families. And, in the process, we stop drinking the bitter poison of unforgiveness—a poison that destroys no one more than ourselves. Even when molesters and abusers do not repent, admit their faults, or ask our forgiveness, we obey God when we forgive them. When we forgive our parents or our children and ask them to forgive us, we drop the pebble. From there, the ripples continue to reach out into the lives of others.

Let's consider some patterns that seem to repeat themselves in contributing to same-sex attractions. If they are present in our own homes, it is our responsibility before

God to make changes—big changes—in obedience to his Word, his ways, and his wisdom. If they are present in the families of others about whom we are concerned, we can take proactive steps toward helping them too. The following section highlights some specific, family-related situations that can increase the likelihood of homosexuality.

> *Most important, I urge you to hold your children before the Lord in fervent prayer throughout their years at home. I am convinced that there is no greater source of confidence and wisdom in parenting. There is not enough knowledge in the books, mine or anyone else's, to counteract the evil that surrounds our kids today. Teenagers are confronted by drugs, alcohol, sex, and foul language wherever they turn. And, of course, the peer pressure on them is enormous. We must bathe them in prayer every day of their lives. The God who made your children will hear your petitions. He has promised to do so. —James Dobson[4]*

How Family Background Influences Sexuality

Parental Attitudes and Style

Classic patterns recur in the background of some homosexual behavior.[5] These patterns usually involve a physically absent or emotionally unavailable father. They can be also attributed to a controlling, domineering, or emotionally dependent mother (see chapter 7).

Physical or verbal abuse and emotional abandonment or rejection can contribute to the sexual confusion of a young boy or girl. A girl born into a family that wanted a boy or vice versa may be programmed by the parents to identify as a

member of the opposite sex. Many highly respected thera-
pists strongly believe that those who choose homosexual
behavior have had a difficult time forming healthy emotional
bonds with their same-sex parent. We will look at all these
factors closely in chapter 7.

On the positive side, parents who are genuinely interested in what their child is learning—drama, science, sports,
arts, or whatever else—will reinforce the child's God-given
identity and build healthy self-esteem. Conversely, parents
who put down or denigrate a child without a healthy balance
of affirmation will cause that child to feel distanced and
rejected. We will provide some principles for building positive family relationships in chapter 6.

Sexual Abuse
Sexual abuse, including molestation and/or rape is a key factor in homosexuality. We will return to this issue repeatedly,
because it is so significant.

Life Crisis
A traumatic episode may be a factor in a young person's gender confusion. A family member's death (especially suicide),
illness, accident, a violent episode, a parental divorce, or the
significant loss of income or position in the community can
be elements in sexual identity problems.

Low Self-Esteem
Many young people who are drawn toward the homosexual
lifestyle are in search of an identity that will make them feel
accepted. When their peers reject them, they may turn
toward extreme styles and behaviors in search of acceptance. Many young people who struggle with gender issues

suffer from disabilities—some as simple as poor vision or hearing, others including deformities, speech impediments, learning disabilities, or other conditions that cause them to be rejected socially or to feel like misfits or outcasts. Most self-esteem problems begin at home.

A Constellation of Causes

Chapter 8 looks at the family and beyond it for contributing factors to the homosexual condition.

What Can We Do?

What are we to do in the face of these factors? No matter if we are parents, youth pastors, counselors, or simply "friends of the family," the first thing we can assume is a loving, accepting attitude. *An absence of love and acceptance is one of the primary contributors to every kind of self-destructive and addictive behavior, including same-sex attraction.*

The next thing we can do is to identify specific concerns and determine realistically how we can make a difference. Great sensitivity to all concerned is important, balanced with a desire to make life better—not worse—for the young person involved. Clearly, we aren't going to walk up to the parents and say, "If you don't get your act together, your son (or daughter) is going to turn into a homosexual." Nor are we going to approach a young boy or girl and tell them we are "worried about your gay tendencies." So what can we do? Are the problems we see situations that can be safely or wisely discussed with the parents? In the case of sexual or physical abuse, there are specific steps that we may be required to take, legally or morally. The following information is essential if someone confides in you about sexual, spousal, or other physical abuse. The following information was specifically written for youth workers, but may be a helpful guide to anyone faced with a confidence of this nature.

When Someone Confides in You

If you talk about sexual abuse enough times, someone will seek you out for help. You will have touched an issue that is never very far from the abused person's mind and heart. Abused people are dealing with their secret with every sermon, relationship, and activity in their lives. If and when they come to you, here are six principles to help you help them:

1. Believe it. Few people lie about sexual abuse. There are occasional false stories, but most often the stories people tell us are all too true. Assume that the person is telling you the truth until proven otherwise.

2. Listen well. Let them tell you their story at their pace. Clarify, but don't interrogate. Abused people need a listening ear. If you have had a similar experience, you may wish to tell them, but do not go on and on with your own story. They need to talk.

3. Be supportive. Sexual abuse victims who tell you about their trauma need your support. They need your verbal assurance that you believe them and will care for them and help them. And they need your time. If God entrusts one of these precious souls to you, you will have to be available to give him or her the priceless gift of your time. Also, in listening to the story, we may be tempted to say things like "that was dumb" or "you shouldn't have been so careless!" Don't be critical! Abused people do not need to be reminded about their mistakes or bad decisions.

---

4. Recognize emotional and medical needs. As someone is telling you his or her story, do not overlook medical or emotional needs. They may need to see a doctor or other professional immediately.

5. Find community resources. Have easily accessible phone numbers for rape crisis hotlines, department of mental health, medical facilities, and women's centers at local colleges and universities. Don't try to handle the problem on your own.

6. Don't keep it a secret. Again—you cannot handle this problem alone! It is a huge mistake not to report sexual abuse to authorities, and getting victims into the system is the best thing you can do. In most states, the law requires you to report sexual or physical abuse. Tell the abused person of your desire to report the crime, and tell him or her that you will walk them through this, keeping in mind the fact that they are most vulnerable and willing to share their problem for about 48 hours, after which they may pull back. Let the proper authorities handle the legal and psychological problems, and you be a friend and/or pastoral counselor. The system is not always perfect, and if you wish, report the abuse to a Christian counselor or therapist, but do not keep it to yourself. If you choose not to report this crime, you are hindering the healing process and perhaps breaking the law.[6]

Steps in the Right Direction

Once we have given thought and prayer to our possible actions, words, or other forms of involvement, there are some helpful and positive things we can do.

1. We can invite a young girl or boy to be around our own family and expose them to appropriate role models in a warm, caring, and affirming environment.

2. We can reinforce healthy sexual roles through compliments, role-specific activities (i.e. one-on-one sports coaching with boys; grooming tips or shopping for feminine clothes with girls), personal conversations, and letting them know of your concern by praying especially for them and with them. Be genuinely interested in whatever catches the attention of specific kids.

3. We can suggest, provide (if we are qualified), or perhaps even finance professional counseling for those who are struggling with critical family problems or with a life crisis resolution (death, family suicide, divorce, or disease).

4. We can make sure that any available medical care is provided for the young person.

5. We can encourage inclusiveness on the part of our own family, the church, the youth group, or any other social environment that may provide emotional support.

6. We can pray. God answers prayer, and even those who are less capable of active involvement in the lives of young people can support the efforts of others through intercessory prayer.

Do nothing out of selfish ambition or vain conceit, but in humility consider others better than yourselves. Each of you should look not only to your own interests, but also to the interests of others. Your attitude should be the same as that of Christ Jesus. (Philippians 2:3–5)

Whenever Kate was at the house, she and Chad prayed for the Sanders family. After a few weeks, Sarah returned to school. She kept to herself, and many of the students avoided her, thanks to the endless gossip and rumors that had been spread during her rehabilitation process.

One afternoon, Chad asked Kate's opinion about an idea: "What would you think about my inviting Brian and Sarah to church? I know that Sarah's rehab was a Christian 12-step program—she told me that herself. And I know Brian would like the worship band, because he plays guitar."

Kate felt a little unsure about Chad's suggestion—she knew the Sanders had kept themselves very isolated since the arrest of the father and that there was a good chance that Brian and Sarah would say no. She was afraid Chad would feel rejected, and that was the last thing he needed. She hesitated, but then agreed. "I think it's a great idea, Chad, but they may be uncomfortable, so don't take it to heart if they say no."

"I know. I already thought about that."

Chad talked to Brian first, and when he said okay, he'd like to hear the band, Chad took a deep breath and talked to Sarah. "Your brother's coming to my church Sunday—I invited him to hear the band. Do you want to come too? Maybe we could all go out to lunch afterwards . . . or something."

"Are you sure you want to be seen with the notorious Sanders kids?" Sarah searched Chad's face carefully.

"I thought maybe you wouldn't want to be seen with a sophomore . . ."

Sarah chuckled. "I guess being a sophomore is almost as bad as being me. Anyway, I'll go if Brian does. He and I need to stick together."

"I . . . I want you to know that I've been praying for you during all the stuff you've been through. My family has some prob-

lems too, so I sort of understood. Anyway, I'm glad you're going . . ."

The next time Chad saw Kate, they prayed together that God would make sure the church visit took place as planned. They also prayed that Sarah and her brother Brian would meet the Lord there and become part of God's Christian family.

"No guarantees," Kate smiled at Chad. "But it's a good place to start."

Chad nodded. "Somebody needs to be nice to them. I sure wouldn't want to be in their shoes. So much for their perfect family. Sad, isn't it?"

"It's the saddest thing in the world."

A Christian home has God's . . .
Sovereignty as its walls and roof,
Truth as its foundation,
Hope as its windows,
Love as its warmth and light,
Faith as its atmosphere,
Joy as its décor, and
Mercy as its doorway to the outside world. [7]

Chapter Three

Homosexuals: Born or Made?

When the classroom conversation turned to homosexuality, Stephanie raised her hand almost immediately. "Why do people make such a big deal out of homosexuality?" she asked impatiently. "Why do we even need to talk about it? You're either gay or you aren't. You're either born that way or you aren't. It's pretty simple, isn't it? So what's the big deal?"

Andrew shook his head emphatically. "You're wrong Stephanie. People are not born gay. They choose to be gay. It's like anything else—you can be anything you want to be in this world, good or bad. It's up to you, and nobody's making the decision for you."

Stephanie had never liked Andrew in the first place, and now that he'd decided to disagree with her, she felt even more annoyed with him than usual. "Look, Andrew, my brother's gay, okay? He says he's always known he's gay, even as a little kid. He wouldn't lie about it. So obviously it's true."

"So what if he started out early? That still doesn't mean he was born that way. In my opinion, people who say that are just looking for excuses . . ."

Stephanie's voice was shrill. "Excuses for what? For the way he is? What's to excuse? I love my brother and as far as I'm concerned he's a better person than . . ."

When he saw how angry both Andrew and Stephanie were becoming, their teacher interrupted. "Hey, c'mon. Let's not get carried away here. I think you both have some interesting things to say, and I'd like to talk more about the subject. But let's be calm and approach it from a factual point of view. How many of you have heard that homosexuality is genetic?"

Almost every hand in the class went up.

The teacher looked around and continued, "And how many of you have heard that the studies that led to that point of view have been called into question, and virtually all of them are now considered to be inconclusive?"

Stephanie interrupted again, "Of course they've been called into question. There are a lot of homophobic people around who just can't accept the facts."

"Stephanie, you're right in saying that we need to look at the facts. That's a given. But let's not jump to any conclusions about what the facts really are."

Andrew raised his hand again. "I just have one question. How can homosexuality be genetic if God says it's wrong?"

Stephanie stood up and looked for all the world like she was going to attack Andrew on the spot. "You're such a know-it-all! How can it be wrong if God made people that way?"

Just as the teacher was about to interrupt again, the bell rang, signaling the end of class. "Great," one of the students remarked as everybody rushed out the door. "That was a big help. I know even less now than I did before class, if that's possible."

Since the mid-1980s, the idea that people are born gay has been widely publicized, primarily because of five specific scientific studies. Any results of these studies that implied a biological reason for homosexuality were reported on television and on the front pages of major newspapers. Their results were published with great interest and excitement, and the studies themselves were applauded as major scientific breakthroughs.

However, as is often the case, questions were later raised about the tests' accuracy, authenticity, or methodology. By then the media was less than enthusiastic about printing follow-up stories. If the disputes were reported at all, these subsequent reports were often filled with complex technical information, and usually were found on the last pages of the newspapers. Most of them were ignored by television and radio.

The consequence of this low-visibility news coverage and follow-up was that it has left many readers—especially those who digest their news in small sound-bytes—with some profoundly false impressions. They are under the impression that scientists have proved, beyond the shadow of a doubt, that homosexuality is determined by DNA codes or by some variation in the brain's structure. In reality, the evidence is inconclusive, and a growing body of critics believes that there is evidence to the contrary.[1]

We should not, as the homespun saying goes, believe everything we read in the newspapers or hear reported on TV . . . Secondly, scientific studies are printed in ink, not etched in stone. —John Harvey[2]

We should bear in mind, as long as people seek physiological and genetic explanations for homosexual behavior, various research reports will continue to surface as headline news stories. It is also worth noting that when these headline stories are discredited by other research, those findings will never be as prominently positioned by the news agencies as the original "breakthrough" reports.

Five Different Stories

In order to give a brief overview of the five key studies that led the public to believe the genetic origin conclusion, I have summarized them. They all involve very complicated biological details and unfamiliar terms, so I have attempted to simplify them as much as possible. I hope you'll bear with me as I try to explain, with minimal complexities, the basic information involved in these studies and some conclusions that can be reached.[3]

Study #1

Let's begin in 1991, when a neurobiologist named Simon Le Vay conducted a study on the differing sizes of the brain's hypothalamus in homosexual males, as opposed to that of heterosexual males and females. He studied six women, sixteen men who were presumed to be heterosexual, and nineteen men who were known to be homosexual. He determined that one specific part of the hypothalamus—a section which has to do with sexual arousal, along with controlling body temperature, sleep, and anger—appeared to be larger in heterosexual men than in homosexuals or females. This specific region seemed to be of a smaller size in men who were known to be homosexual.

Le Vay's was a very small study. It was disputed by other

scientists, some of whom questioned the likelihood that the supposedly heterosexual males tested were, in fact, AIDS victims.[4] Le Vay himself stated, "sexual orientation in humans is amenable to study at a biological level . . . further interpretation of the results of this study must be considered speculative." But despite Le Vay's own disclaimers, the study was widely reported as "proof" of inborn homosexuality. The questions it raised were not publicized.

Study #2
The following year, in 1992, Laura Allen and Robert Gorski studied the size of a different part of the brain. They examined around two hundred autopsied brains, and they found that there was a difference between homosexual males and heterosexual males and females in the size of the *anterior commissure*. Although that part of the brain is not known to relate to sexual function, they proposed that it might have some general impact on cognitive function. This, they thought, might make an overall difference in sexual orientation.

One of the problems with this test was the great variation of sizes within each group. For example, some of the women's *anterior commissure* measurements were three times that of other women, and only the average sizes produced the reported differences. Questions were also raised about the effect of the AIDS virus upon the brains that were analyzed—AIDS frequently afflicts brain tissue and could affect its size.

Like Le Vay's work, the Allen/Gorski study received front-page attention. The subsequent questions it raised, most of them emanating from the scientific community itself, received barely a mention.

*Sexual orientation is not like a birthmark, something
capable of clear, external verification. Rather it is part of a
person's subjective self-perception. By definition, that is
something that cannot be assigned without consent.*
—David Link[5]

Study #3

Also in 1991, J. M. Bailey and R. Pillard carried out another
well-known study on the possible genetic cause of homosexuality. They interviewed 56 homosexual males who were
identical twins, 54 homosexual males who had fraternal twin
brothers, and 57 homosexual males who had adoptive brothers. They found that 52 percent of the identical co-twins were
also homosexual, compared to 22 percent of the fraternal co-
twins, and 11 percent of the adoptive brothers.

Although this study indicated that there was a higher
percentage of homosexuals among the identical twins, that
percentage was just slightly more than half. That means that
almost half of the identical twin brothers were heterosexual.
Since identical twins share the same genetic code, it would
seem that this test was more conclusively *against* a genetic
cause for homosexuality than confirming such a cause. Yet
this twin study has been touted as another reason to believe
that homosexuality is inborn.

Study #4

One well-publicized study, which took place in 1993, was carried out by Dean Hamer. This study focused on the DNA and
on specific markers in one region of the X-chromosome. The
same genetic markers were found in 33 out of 40 homosexual brothers tested, thus indicating that DNA determines

homosexuality. Of course the fact that there were 7 brothers who *did not* have the same genetic pattern raises questions. As John Harvey writes, "If the Hamer study identifies a genetic basis for homosexuality, how is it that seven of the forty brothers' pairs did not show this genetic pattern?"[6]

Another scientist, Dr. Ruth Hubbard, has brought the Hamer test under scrutiny because it did not use a control group. Subsequent tests, similar to Hamer's, by Canadian geneticist George Ebers found no linkage whatsoever between sexual preference and the genetic markers in question.

Study #5

Finally, in 1995 researcher H. Meyer-Bahlburg, who specializes in hormone studies, investigated a possible link between *in utero* exposure to a synthetic estrogen called DES, which is known to interfere with normal estrogen production. The test was meant to determine whether prenatal DES exposure had any effect upon bisexual or same-sex attractions. Comparisons were made between women exposed to DES, their unexposed sisters, and other unrelated women who were also unexposed.

The media widely reported that there was a significantly higher rate of homosexual daydreams, night dreams, as well as sexual attraction and involvement among the women who were exposed to DES. What was not reported, however, was that most of the women were bisexual, not homosexual, and much of what they reported involved their fantasy life and did not translate into actual sexual relations. The researchers themselves concluded that there are many different factors, both biological and sociological, which influence sexual preference.

*The homosexual publication The Advocate asked its readers,
"Do you think sexual orientation is fluid or fixed over a
person's lifetime?" Only 46 percent said yes, they were
born that way. Forty-one percent said sexual orientation is
changeable, and 13 percent said, "We're all bisexual." More
than half of those who responded indicated that sexual
orientation is a choice.[7]*

We've already acknowledged that many factors contribute to homosexuality, and we are well aware that some of
these are biological. But, at the same time, there is no "third
gender" determined by genes or chromosomes, so how can
genetics make any difference whatsoever? Jeffrey Satinover
provides this helpful comparison:

No genes exist that code anyone for becoming a basketball
player. But some genes code for height and the elements of
athleticism, such as quick reflexes, favorable bone structure,
height-to-weight ratio, muscle strength and refresh rate,
metabolism and energy efficiency . . . Someone born with a
favorable (for basketball) combination of height and athleticism is in no way genetically programmed or forced to
become a basketball player. These qualities, however, certainly facilitate that choice. As a consequence the choice to
play basketball has a clear genetic component . . .[8]

It is in this sense that homosexuality can result from a
constellation of factors. And it is in this same sense that
homosexuality is preventable.

Stephanie was still fuming about the class discussion when she got home from school. "You wouldn't believe what a jerk Andrew is," she told her mother. "He says homosexuals are that way because they want to be. Can you believe it?"

"Well, some homosexuals agree with him," Stephanie's mom explained. "There are a lot of gays and lesbians out there who don't want anyone telling them that they had no choice about their sexuality."

"Why would they feel like that? If they don't have to be gay, why would they want to be?"

"That's exactly the kind of statement that they reject. They feel being gay is a good choice, and they don't want to be seen as victims—like they have a birth defect or some other abnormality."

"But hasn't Jake always said he was born that way? That's what he told me."

"Stephanie, it's a little more complicated than you think. Jake will be the first to tell you that people have a lot of different reasons for getting involved in the gay community. After all, we're talking about 10 percent of the population."

"10 percent? That's a lot of people, Mom. Are you sure that's right?"

"That's what I've always been told—10 percent, although, come to think of it, I'm not sure how they know. I guess it's just common knowledge."

Everybody's Doing It

Many otherwise well-informed westerners hold yet another false impression about homosexuality. Like Stephanie's mother, they have been led to believe that 10 percent of the population is homosexual. This percentage was part of the famous report by Alfred C. Kinsey, published in 1948 under the title *Sexual Behavior in the Human Male*. The first such popular in-depth study of human sexuality, Kinsey's was a landmark book which changed forever the popular view of sexual behavior among Americans.

Although he is still quoted as a reliable source of well-documented information, there are some serious problems with Kinsey's research. First of all, a fourth of his subjects were prisoners or ex-convicts, some of whom were sex offenders. This clearly does not represent the average American male population.

More recently, Kinsey's own sexual eccentricities have been investigated and reported. He was himself, in fact, a homosexual. For decades, he was personally involved in bizarre experimental sexual behavior. Although he was married and was the father of children, he was nonetheless a sexual eccentric and adventurer who had a particular attraction toward masochism. Interestingly, Alan Gregg of the Rockefeller Foundation stated in the preface to Kinsey's first book that the work was "without moral bias or prejudice." Nothing could have been further from the truth.[9]

The percentage of homosexuals among the population may seem like an insignificant fact. What difference does it make whether 1 percent (which may be closer to the truth[10]) or 10 percent of Americans are actively homosexual? Perhaps it isn't important to most adults, but our concern is with prevention of homosexuality among adolescents, and a statistic of that sort could make a significant difference to a young girl or boy who is struggling with same-sex attraction. The fewer people that are actually involved, the less "normal" the homosexual lifestyle seems to outside observers. The fact is, very few people actually have adopted an active homosexual lifestyle. As vocal as some members of the homosexual community are, they really represent a very small, very marginal group of people.

Young people are probably more influenced by the media than any other segment of the population. And it isn't just inaccurate facts and statistics that deceive them. They are continuously bombarded with music, videos, films, and interviews with celebrities which tell them, again and again, that any form of sexuality a la mode is a perfectly acceptable and normal role for them. The kinkiness of Dennis Rodman, the overt lesbianism of K. D. Lang, the "outing" of Ellen Degeneres, the eerie androgyny of Michael Jackson, the "finally healthy" homosexuality of Elton John—the list is long, and the exposure to sexually unorthodox individuals is relentless. It must seem to teens that at least half the population is involved in "alternative" sexuality.

⤚

A POPULAR MYTH: Homosexual behavior is genetic—or like a third gender.

Consider this: Homosexual feelings are developed by a complex group of circumstances in life, set up over a period of time from birth to one's early years. Later in life, these feelings play a role in choices one makes involving sexual relations with others. Because all sexual behavior is learned behavior, a person may be inclined, because of feelings, to homosexual behavior. The choice may, in addition, be motivated by social rejection, physical or emotional disabilities, hormonal imbalances, sexual abuse, or poor role modeling. Just as people with a tendency for alcoholism must be responsible for their drinking choices, so people with a tendency toward homosexual behavior should be responsible for their sexual choices.

A growing number of spokespersons for the homosexual community reject the idea of being "born that way." Celtic violinist Ashley Mac Isaac says, "For me, homosexuality is a learned behavior. I don't think it could be a genetic trait. We're born for reproduction so that life can continue."[11]

Lesbian writer Jennifer Terry reports, "A gay social worker who works with suicidal teens told me recently that the biology-is-destiny line can be deadly. Thinking they are 'afflicted' with homosexual desire as a kind of disease or biological defect, rather than it being a desire they somehow choose, is, for many gay teenagers, one more reason to commit suicide rather than to live in a world hostile to their desires."[12]

This mirrors the view of psychiatrist and author Charles Socarides, who observes, " . . . It is not a kindness to homosexuals to attribute their serious disturbance in psychosexual development to organicity. It dooms them to a life which is extraterritorial to the biological and social realities which surround them."[13]

Although we must always emphasize our Christian love toward others, we must also remind ourselves and those we love that God has made some fairly clear statements about sexuality. To sum up his point of view, God created sex to take place between a male and female who are married to each other. He designed sexuality primarily for procreation, but also for pleasure. And, within the boundaries established in his Word, he didn't provide any alternatives (1 Corinthians 6:9–11).

Once we have established that homosexuality is not an inborn trait, we raise the issue of choices. Since we're talking about adolescents, the subject of making wise and responsible decisions isn't exactly a new topic of conversation. We've probably already talked about it regarding drugs, alcohol, safe-driving, premarital heterosexual sex, and eating disorders. Along similar lines and for many of the same reasons, we also need to discuss good choices in the context of gender identity and homosexuality.

Andrew was still mad about his confrontation with Stephanie. More than anything else, he thought she was incredibly ignorant. He had grown up in a Christian home, he had attended church his entire life, and he certainly knew right from wrong. As far as Andrew was concerned, nothing was more offensive to God than homosexuality.

That afternoon, the phone was ringing when he got home from school. His girlfriend Cara attended a different high school, but she went to his church. Andrew started to tell her about his argument with Stephanie, but Cara interrupted excitedly. "Guess what? My parents are gone for two days. They left for the airport half-an-hour ago. Why don't you come over? The lady who's going to stay with me won't get here 'til seven."

Andrew practically flew out the door. He and Cara rarely had any time together alone, and he was more than ready to take advantage of her parents' absence. When he arrived at her house, Cara was in her swimsuit. He could hardly keep his eyes off her—she was amazing.

"Let's use the spa," she smiled. "It's a perfect day for it."

They hadn't been in the warm bubbles for more than five minutes before they were kissing, then they were petting, and very soon one thing led to another. By the time an hour had passed, Andrew and Cara had become too sexually involved to stop themselves. For the first time in either of their lives, they had sexual intercourse.

That evening, Andrew was exceptionally quiet, and his parents wanted to know why. "Oh," he lied, "I'm still upset about an argument I had at school."

"About what?" His dad looked up curiously.

"Well, Stephanie's brother Jake is gay, and she was trying to tell us that homosexuality is genetic—that people are born that way. I told her that if God says it's wrong then it's pretty lame to say that people can't help it. It's a sin. Period. Right?"

"Right, it's a sin. And I guess if anything is genetic, it's our human inclination to sin. It's part of who we are, but that doesn't mean we can't help it. It doesn't matter what the sin is— stealing, lying, having sex outside of marriage, or homosexuality—it's all sin. And God expects better of us."

"Dad, you're not trying to say that homosexuality is the same as premarital sex, are you?"

"It may have different consequences, but as far as God's concerned, one sin is about the same as another. James 2:10 says, 'Whoever keeps the whole law and yet stumbles at just one point is guilty of breaking all of it.'"

"Really?"

"Really."

Andrew stared at his plate. He didn't dare look at either of his parents. His mother could read him like a book. And as far as his father was concerned, if he even imagined what had happened that afternoon . . .

"Interesting. Well, I've got some homework ..." Andrew vanished into his room and shut the door.

All the pleasure of his experience with Cara was gone. He felt guilty and afraid.

At least I'm not gay, *he reminded himself.*

But somehow, after what his dad had said, even that didn't give him much comfort.

Unless we acknowledge that we are all in need of God's grace and healing in our sexuality, we will continue to prevent homosexuals and others from listening to us, because they will hear only our fear and revulsion, not our love and similar need.—Thomas E. Schmidt [14]

The Truth about Consequences

Like Andrew, most people don't put homosexual behavior in the same category as premarital sex. Although some sins seem to be less harmful than others, the Bible states that the ultimate result of all sin is death (Romans 6:23). It is true that the life expectancy of a young homosexual is gravely lower than that of a heterosexual of the same age (more about this in chapter 5). The suicide rate among those who practice homosexual behavior is higher than it is among heterosexuals; death strikes more frequently due to disease, violence, and suicide. If we are concerned about the dangers of smoking and substance abuse, we should also be concerned about the death risks inherent in homosexual behavior.

However, the possibility of death resulting from out-of-wedlock sex is clearly a risk too, most notably to an unborn child (because of abortion). Premarital sex can also endanger the life of the mother, who may be ill-prepared for pregnancy and childbirth. Children born to unwed mothers, particularly to teenagers, are at higher risk of child abuse due to huge emotional and financial stresses. Besides all the physical risks, there are countless dreams that die in the midst of an unplanned teenage pregnancy. Even the joyful birth of a baby is overshadowed by heartbreaking losses.

The unloving treatment of "sinners"—the kind of judgmental behavior Andrew demonstrated toward Stephanie's brother—is clearly an ungodly behavior and it, too, is risky business. A Christian who rejects a young man or woman with homosexual traits, mannerisms, or other tendencies has the responsibility of sending that person back out into a world that offers few safe and godly options. That young person's next stop may be the homosexual community. To the struggling person, homosexual or not, the rejection of Christians usually represents the rejection of God and may cause him or her to turn away from Christ and Christians once and for all.

Galatians 6:7 says, "Do not be deceived: God cannot be mocked. A man reaps what he sows. The one who sows to please his sinful nature, from that nature will reap destruction; the one who sows to please the Spirit, from the Spirit will reap eternal life." According to this scripture, there are consequences for our behavior. This does not mean that God punishes us. Nor does it mean that God doesn't forgive our sins. It simply means that there are inevitable effects resulting from our choices.

Let me give you an example that strikes very close to home. When I was a young man, I was warned repeatedly not to touch the family's farm machinery while it was running. But I found out that I could complete certain tasks more quickly by leaving the machinery running while I serviced it.

Even though I had been told time and again not to do so, I continued to "save time" this way.

One day I caught one of my fingers in the machinery. Instantly and painfully, my finger was cut off. Although no one was angry or judgmental about the accident, my finger was gone forever. This was not "punishment." It was, however, the consequence of my refusal to take good advice and to follow rules that were made for my protection and safety. Even though I was loved and forgiven, my finger will never grow back.

Taking The Humble Approach

When we begin to communicate sexual responsibility to others, we'd better begin by taking a long, hard look at ourselves. Are our own sexual lives being lived in conformity to God's biblical standards? Just about every person alive has committed some kind of sexual sin in thought, word, or deed. If we are somehow continuing in a habit pattern that is inappropriate for a Christian, our first task is to repent—to do an about-face—to approach God for forgiveness, and to seek from his Spirit and from his Word the strength to overcome our temptations (Psalm 119:59–60). This, of course, places us in a position of humility, not of superiority. And that is the only position from which we are able to successfully minister to others.

Once the humility issue is addressed, we have several things to communicate to the young people we care about—whether they are our own children, friends, acquaintances, members of a youth group, counselees, or simply young women or men who have crossed our path. There are some important principles that we can share with them, and I believe they can be listed as follows, bearing in mind that our first priority in life is a right, active, and committed relationship with Jesus Christ. The Gospel is our primary message.

1. Sex between males and females is a wonderful thing, but it is intended to be enjoyed only within marriage.
2. Same-sex emotional attractions are not sinful, but they can open the door to same-sex actions. It is easier to stop same-sex attractions before they get a stronghold in the young person's mind, rather than wait until they have progressed to overt homosexual behavior.
3. Many homosexuals suffer from addictive behaviors, including sexual addictions. And the family, lifestyle, and personal problems that lead to compulsive behavior and to drug and alcohol abuse are the same problems that can contribute to homosexuality. If we aren't afraid to reach out to the kids who are fighting a day-to-day battle with drinking, substance abuse, or eating disorders, why should we be any less committed to the boys and girls who struggle with same-sex attractions? Then once we've overcome our fear, how do we deal with them?

Here are four scriptures that address our proper attitude toward people with behavior problems. Consider these statements:

- **1 Corinthians 16:13-14:** "Be on your guard; stand firm in the faith; be men of courage; be strong. Do everything in love."

- **Psalm 116:5:** "The LORD is gracious and righteous; our God is full of compassion."

- **Matthew 7:12:** God's Golden Rule—treat others as you want to be treated.

- **Matthew 7:1:** "Do not judge, or you too will be judged."

As we consider the alternatives to adopting a loving, compassionate, and nonjudgmental spirit, we really have but one option. God's Word has shown us that homosexuality, like drinking, doing drugs, having premarital sex, and every other kind of self-destructive behavior, is a choice. It is a personal decision, not a predetermined destiny. When we choose to move away from God's best, we set ourselves up for tragic consequences. In the pages to come, we'll explore some of the ways followers of Jesus can best demonstrate unconditional love.

Meanwhile, we would be wise to remember our own imperfections as we reach out to others in their own needs and weaknesses. Whenever we think we are strong, our weaknesses have a way of resurfacing, in a more destructive manner than before. Perhaps every one of us who chooses to be involved in the prevention and transformation of inappropriate sexual behavior—homosexual or heterosexual—should engrave this motto upon our hearts: *There, but for the grace of God, go I.*

Andrew stood next to Stephanie during break, and for a few moments he was afraid to open his mouth. Finally, he managed to blurt out the little speech he'd been rehearsing for a week: "Stephanie, I think I owe you an apology."

"For what?" Her voice was cold.

"For insulting your brother that day in class. I was judging him, and I have no business doing that. I'm no better than he is."

Stephanie wasn't sure what to make of Andrew's weird behavior. "Uh, okay. But why are you telling me this? I don't get it."

"I'm just apologizing to you. That's all there is to it. I'm sorry."

Having completed his mission, Andrew quickly withdrew from the scene. Stephanie watched him go in silence.

"What's up with him?" her friend Julie asked.

"I'm not sure. He's been acting a lot nicer since his girlfriend dumped him."

"What girlfriend?"

"Oh, Cara. The one from his church. They broke up a couple of weeks ago. Not that I blame her. Can you imagine going out with him? He's so incredibly self-righteous."

"I thought you said he apologized."

"Yeah, he did. So what?"

"So . . . he must be sorry."

"Yeah. Must be." Stephanie stared at Andrew's back as he walked away. She was thoroughly bewildered by his new attitude. Sorry? Andrew? Must be something he picked up at church, she finally concluded, pulling several books out of her locker, and slamming the door even more loudly than usual.

Chapter Four

What Would Jesus Say?

To put it mildly, Maryanne and her mother weren't seeing eye to eye. Maryanne was sixteen years old, and she had been elected junior class president at her high school. Besides participating in the usual student body activities, her idea of being a good class president meant trying to "help" her fellow students with their problems. Of course it was a kind and loving idea. But over a period of two months, Maryanne's grades were spiraling downward, her phone was ringing at all hours of the night, and worst of all (for her mother, at least), she had become the "defender" of every underdog in the eleventh grade.

Maryanne's family belonged to a large, thriving community church, and they were all very involved in its various activities. Maryanne's mother had always felt safe about the friends her daughter made at church because they seemed like such nice, wholesome kids. But now, with this new role of "rescuer," Maryanne was spending hours with school friends who, in her mom's opinion, didn't belong in any church, and certainly not in theirs.

The worst of them all was Stephen. He'd transferred in from another high school, and on his first day of school, Stephen had informed anyone who would listen that he was bisexual. Sure he liked girls. But he liked boys too. He was flamboyant, he wore wild clothes, and he had some very theatrical mannerisms. In fact, when Maryanne told her mother about Stephen, the older woman rolled her eyes and said, "Just don't bring the little pervert over here."

Maryanne's temper had flared. "How dare you call him that? He's a human being just like anybody else. You have no right . . ."

Maryanne's mother had a temper too. Before long, the conversation had escalated into a screaming match. The more her mother disapproved of Stephen, the more Maryanne defended him. Finally, in desperation, Maryanne said, "Maybe I should take him to church. If he's such a terrible person, maybe he needs God."

Her mother's face paled, and she was momentarily speechless. Finally, she said, "You take him to our church, and I'll find another one."

The more she thought about it, the more appealing the idea was to Maryanne. The next Sunday, she and Stephen showed up in Sunday school. Her mom had called Jim Cline, the youth director, to "warn" him, so when Stephen and Maryanne walked in, Jim had already thought about his response.

"This is Stephen, Jim. He's a good friend of mine."

Jim's big smile and warm handshake took Stephen by surprise. "I'm so glad you could come," Jim greeted him. "I'm looking forward to getting to know you."

Jim was the kind of youth pastor who believed in accepting kids "as is." He didn't allow drinking, drugs, bad language, or other inappropriate behavior in the church, but he had a strong belief that kids should be loved unconditionally. So that's what he'd decided to do about "the Stephen situation," as Maryanne's mother called it.

But once Stephen began to attend, Maryanne's mother insisted that the family leave the church and go elsewhere. Another major fight took place, and eventually, it was agreed that Maryanne could go to church wherever she wanted. So she and Stephen continued to attend the community church services. Before many months had passed, Stephen began to change—for the better. He stopped trying to shock people, stopped advertising his sexual ideas, and finally, he started talking to Jim about becoming a Christian.

"I really want to be at peace with God. But do I have to stop being bisexual?" he asked.

Jim shook his head. "I think you should come to Jesus just the way you are. He'll show you what he wants in his own good time."

When Maryanne's mother heard about this, she called up the church pastor and demanded that he fire Jim Cline. "Don't you know what the Bible says?" she demanded. "It says no homosexual will enter the Kingdom of God. How can you allow that fool to run your youth group? He's going to corrupt every one of those nice kids. If you let him stay, you ought to be fired too!"

W HEN IT COMES TO HOMOSEXUALITY, there is a dramatic polarization in the Christian church. There are people, like Maryanne's mother, who won't give a moment's consideration to gender confusion or adolescent sexual identity issues. "Sin is sin!" they'll tell you, and as far as they're concerned, there is simply no room for discussion. On the other side of the fence are Christians who claim, through some rather curious biblical interpretations, that the Bible has no problem with homosexuals. They are convinced that the Scriptures which are often cited against homosexuality are misunderstood, taken out of historical context, or written by uptight prudes.

What Am I Supposed to Think?

Some churches and denominations are making decisions to ordain homosexual ministers and priests. Some are devising "marriage" ceremonies for same-sex couples. Some are reinterpreting Holy Scriptures to be "inclusive" of all alternative lifestyles. And some are claiming that Jesus himself was a homosexual.

On the other side of the ledger are individuals who consider homosexuality to be the most offensive sin of all. These people believe that, in order to become real Christians, homosexuals must repent every aspect of their same-sex attraction and homosexual condition before they can pray for salvation through the work of Christ on the cross. One youth pastor, when asked what he would do if a homosexual came into his youth group, said, "I know what I *should* do, but I also know what I *feel* like doing. I'd feel like beating the 'queer' out of him."

Somewhere between these two poles are individuals of various other opinions. Some are highly supportive of ex-gay movements such as Exodus, Courage, and Homosexuals Anonymous. Churchgoers may feel it is necessary for them to condemn homosexuality in general, but still maintain their own personal tolerance. There are those who are deeply confused and ambivalent. And, most painful of all, there are parents, siblings, and even children whose loved ones have chosen to pursue a homosexual lifestyle. These people feel marginalized by other Christians, they feel cut off from their homosexual loved ones, and as far as the Bible is concerned, they have no idea what they are supposed to believe.

What Did Jesus Really Say?

People sometimes point out that Jesus never addressed the issue of homosexuality. He did, however, speak of human sexuality according to God's design:

> "Haven't you read . . . that at the beginning the Creator 'made them male and female,' and said, 'For this reason a man will leave his father and mother and be united to his wife, and the two will become one flesh'? So they are no longer two, but one. Therefore what God has joined together, let man not separate." (Matthew 19:4–6)

Although Jesus was addressing the question of divorce, he was also stating God's original intention for marriage and the family. Clearly, throughout Scripture, marriage is defined as a relationship between a man and a woman. There is no biblical precedent for same-sex marriages or for same-sex physical intimacy.

But it is very important for us to note that Scripture leaves no room for heterosexual intimacy outside of marriage, either. It does not condone premarital sex, nor does it make allowances for what we call adultery—sexual activity between men or women who are married to someone else. In fact, the same statement is made about adulterers, drunks, and cheats as is made about homosexuals. The apostle Paul writes,

> Do you not know that the wicked will not inherit the kingdom of God? Do not be deceived: Neither the sexually

immoral nor idolaters nor adulterers nor male prostitutes nor
homosexual offenders nor thieves nor the greedy nor drunk-
ards nor slanderers nor swindlers will inherit the kingdom of
God. (1 Corinthians 6:9–10)

Our first guideline as we approach the Bible's view of any
sin is to remember that *we are all prone to sin*. The reason we
Christians have a relationship with God is not because we are
sin-free. It is because we have faced up to the reality of our
sinful nature and have received God's pardon through the
life, death, and resurrection of Jesus Christ. That and that
alone makes us worthy of eternal life. "All have sinned and
fall short of the glory of God" (Romans 3:23); and by grace
we are saved (Ephesians 2:8).

A POPULAR MYTH: According to the Bible,
homosexuality is okay.

Consider this:

Leviticus 20:13: "If a man lies with a man as one lies
with a woman, both of them have done what is
detestable."

Leviticus 18:22: "Do not lie with a man as one lies
with a woman; that is detestable."

1 Corinthians 6:9: "Neither the sexually immoral
nor idolaters nor adulterers nor male prostitutes nor
homosexual offenders . . . will inherit the kingdom of
God."

Romans 1:26–27: "God gave them over to shameful
lusts. Even their women exchanged natural relations
for unnatural ones. In the same way the men also
abandoned natural relations with women and were
inflamed with lust for one another. Men committed

indecent acts with other men, and received in themselves the due penalty for their perversion."

As firm and clear as these Scriptures are, the Bible also says that we are to love one another, we are not to judge one another, and we are to demonstrate compassion and mercy along with our expressions of morality. Christians are to be known for their love and treating others as they expect to be treated, not for their self-righteous, rule-keeping perfectionism. So even as we accept the biblical judgments against homosexual behavior, we must simultaneously accept the biblical requirements that we love the person taken in sin, even though we are offended, frightened, or even repulsed by his or her sin.

Lorraine, Maryanne's mother, made an appointment with the pastor, and she had every intention of secretly recording their conversation, taking the tape to the church's board of elders, and demanding the poor man's immediate resignation. But the very day Lorraine was scheduled to meet with the pastor, she received a call from Maryanne's friend Stephen. "I want to talk to you," he explained. "Can I come to your home?"

"What do you want to talk to me about?" she snapped at him, convinced he was manipulating her for some twisted reason.

"I . . . I want you to know about my relationship with Jesus," he stammered, painfully unsure of himself.

Lorraine started to make a rude comment, but something stopped her. He was probably trying to con her, but what if he wasn't? She didn't want to be guilty of turning him away if he had truly met Christ. Opinionated as she was, Lorraine wasn't without some understanding of spiritual things.

"Is Maryanne with you?"

"No, she doesn't know I'm calling you. She'd probably be . . . well, you know . . . upset."

That was a surprise. Whatever this was, it wasn't about Maryanne. "When did you want to see me? Right now would be best for me."

"I'll be right over."

Lorraine hadn't seen Stephen for several weeks, and she was amazed by his new appearance. He looked, well, normal. His burgundy hair had grown out to a natural dishwater blond shade. It was neatly trimmed and he was dressed in typical teenage clothes. Nervously, he stood in the doorway, unsure if he should move any farther into the house.

"Come in and sit down," Lorraine instructed him, not unkindly. "What's on your mind?"

"Well, I'm not sure where to start. I guess I want to apologize, first. I was acting pretty psychotic when I met you. I was playing that bisexual game and being totally weird."

Stephen paused, and since Lorraine didn't trust herself to speak, he went on with his story. "I was very confused. In the other school I attended, I had no friends, and the only way I could get anyone to talk to me was by saying off-the-wall things and acting crazy. So I just started playing different roles and freaking everybody out. For awhile, I really did think I might be gay. I mean, guys hated me because I was such a terrible athlete. Girls liked me better because I could relate to them about feelings, and I love the theatre, and so I guess I thought, maybe, I was supposed to be born a girl or something . . ."

"That's ridiculous, Stephen. Anyone can see that you're a boy."

"I mean on the inside—or at least that's what I thought I meant—but since I started going to church and learning about God and how much he cares for me, I realized that he hadn't

made a mistake when he created me. That's what Jim Cline taught me. He helped me see that I was exactly the way I was supposed to be, except that I was confused. So he prayed with me, and he talked to me about being 'God's man.' At first I didn't know what he was talking about, but he just meant living up to the ideal of manhood that God intended for me."

He stopped for a breath, then burst out, "Am I making any sense?"

Lorraine felt terribly ashamed of herself, but she wasn't quite ready to admit it. After all, it might just be an act of some kind. "So have you invited Jesus Christ to be your personal Savior?" she asked, her voice sounding more curt than she intended.

Stephen answered with the most amazing smile, "Yes! That's what I wanted you to know! I've come to know the Lord, and he's changing me so much I can't even believe I'm the same person. I do want you to know one thing, though . . ."

"What's that?"

"I want you to know that although I talked about bisexuality, I'd never actually . . . I mean I hadn't really been with another guy. It was just talk . . ."

Lorraine felt even worse, but instead of apologizing, she just smiled at Stephen and said, "I'm really happy for you, Steve. I can see how much you've changed, and it's pretty obvious that God gets the credit. You couldn't have changed that much by yourself."

"Well, I did have to cooperate . . ."

At last, Lorraine was defeated, "Steve, of course you cooperated. Look, I owe you a big apology. I judged you for what you said about yourself instead of looking beyond your disguise and seeing your need. I'm really happy that you wanted to talk to me. It took a lot of courage on your part, and I wouldn't have blamed you if you'd never spoken to me again."

"Well, I don't blame you, either. Maryanne is one of the most wonderful people I've ever met, and I know you wanted to protect her from getting into some kind of a mess. That's what mothers are for, you know."

Once they'd completed their conversation, Stephen left. Lorraine quickly went to the phone and called the church. "Yes, I'd like to cancel my meeting with Pastor Dixon. No, there's no reason to reschedule. It's fine. Thanks anyway."

So Everything Is Okay, Right?

Stephen turned away from homosexuality before it changed—in his case—from a head game to a physical experience. It was easier for him because he had no relationships to cut off, no physical pleasures to abandon, no unfulfilled longings to leave behind. But it's important to realize that the more involved young men and women become in homosexual activities, the more difficult it is for them to repent and "go straight." Some who have come out of the homosexual lifestyle after becoming Christians have warned those who mentor them, "I'll never be normal— I've got too much baggage. Don't expect too much from me."

One of the most challenging questions Christians must face has to do with the tension that exists between "grace" and "works." As Christians we should know that we're unable to overcome our inclination to sin, so the first thing we have to do is ask God to change us from the inside. As he does his work on our hearts, we cooperate by developing self-discipline and by crying out for his help when we are powerfully tempted. This is the way we are "transformed by the renewing of our minds."

> *Therefore, I urge you, brothers, in view of God's mercy, to offer your bodies as living sacrifices, holy and pleasing to God—this is your spiritual act of worship. Do not conform any longer to the pattern of this world, but be transformed by the renewing of your mind. Then you will be able to test and approve what God's will is—his good, pleasing and perfect will. (Romans 12:1–2)*

The tension exists in the fact that sin is deadly, dangerous, and destructive. We can be kind to sinners—even to ourselves as people who are prone to sin—but, at the same time, we have to see sin for what it is. It is a terminal "disease" that separates us from God. Not only does it damage our relationship with him, but its consequences also destroy our lives emotionally, spiritually, and sometimes physically. Sin is evil. Sin is poisonous. Sin is corrosive. And although we are called to love people who are caught in sin even as we love ourselves, we are also called to hate sin in all its variegated forms.

This brings us to a pivotal point in our consideration of homosexuality, particularly as we look at it in the context of Christianity. In another chapter, we will explore the countless and unavoidable risks—extraordinarily dangerous consequences—that accompany homosexual behavior. For now, we will consider the spiritual issues that it encompasses.

If we choose to practice homosexual acts or to participate in the homosexual lifestyle, is everything all right between God and ourselves? The answer, according to Scripture, has to be a resounding no. It's not all right. Forgiven, perhaps. But not all right.

How can we say this? Because the Bible is painfully clear about the issue. Despite arguments raised by homosexual churches and advocates of the "gay" lifestyle, there is no doubt about its meaning. There are several scriptures that address homosexuality very directly. The first time it is mentioned is in Genesis 19:1–9.

Those who defend homosexuality deny that the sin that brought God's judgment upon Sodom was the sin of homosexuality. Some even imply that the great sin of the city was inhospitality, based on Jesus' remarks that the cities that rejected the ministry of his disciples would be worse off than Sodom (Matthew 10:14–15).

It took less than five minutes for me to delude myself into thinking that homosexuality was acceptable to God. It would take another five years before I was willing to reconsider. —Joe Dallas[1]

There were other sins in Sodom besides homosexuality. When we read Romans chapter 1, we see that homosexuality is the culmination of an idolatrous lifestyle, a consequence of worshipping "the created things rather than the Creator." From the brief profile we have in Genesis, Sodom was clearly a self-gratifying, self-worshipping society. But above all its other vices, the description Scripture uses to describe Sodom leaves little to the imagination about the sexual corruption of its inhabitants. Whatever else God had against the men there, the issue he underscores in his Word was their aggressive, uncontrollable lust for the two angels who visited the city. That behavior was detestable to him.

In fact, the Hebrew law says precisely that. In Leviticus 18:22 we read, "Do not lie with a man as one lies with a woman; that is detestable." Leviticus 20:13 goes on to say, "If there is a man who lies with a male as those who lie with a woman, both of them have committed a detestable act; they shall surely be put to death. Their bloodguiltiness is upon them" (NASB).

The argument against this law being relevant to our world goes something like this: That rule was made for a special time, when God was building up a nation. He's not doing that anymore, so it no longer applies. It goes into the same receptacle as the kosher diet, the keeping of the Sabbath, and other culturally and historically irrelevant traditions.

The writings of the apostle Paul, which directly reject homosexual acts as sin (Romans 1:26–27; 1 Corinthians 6:9) are sometimes interpreted as statements about pagan homosexual prostitution rather than referring to homosexual behavior in general. Peter J. Gomes, preacher to Harvard University and author of *The Good Book*, discusses this. He writes, "The homosexuality Paul would have known and to which he makes reference in his letters, particularly to the Romans, has to do with pederasty and male prostitution, and he particularly condemns those heterosexual men and women who assume homosexual practices . . . All Paul knew of homosexuality was the debauched pagan expression of it. He cannot be condemned for that ignorance, but neither should his ignorance be an excuse for our own." [2]

Dr. Gomes's interpretation is incompatible with the belief in the God-breathed inspiration of the Scripture. Whether Paul knew about all the varieties of homosexuality or not, God surely did—and does. And the point remains, from Genesis through Revelation, there is not one positive reference to homosexual behavior. It is always rejected as a form of sinful behavior.

We can and should reach out in love to the homosexual women and men who are part of our lives. We are responsible before God to pray for them, to care for them, to lay down our lives for them if necessary. But we are not called to pretend that their chosen sexual behavior is acceptable to God. Nor are we called to submit to the political agenda to which they, or the organizations to which they belong, subscribe.

Not long after Stephen came to know Christ and began a new life, he attended a sex education assembly at his high school. The film the students watched did not encourage chastity, but instead described in detail the importance of condoms, and even provided instructions about how to use them. This wasn't especially surprising to Stephen; he'd been in public school all his life and didn't expect anything else. But the second part of the film stunned him. It described the affectionate relationship between two high school boys and went on to say that they were homosexual lovers. The script explained that they were born that way, they would always be that way, and they should express their "love" for each other freely—and safely.

The sequence ended with a happy-go-lucky group of students, the two boys as well as a pair of girls who were holding hands, and an assortment of heterosexual couples. Later on, Stephen described the film to Jim Cline. "The message was like 'We're so cool, we're all having sex the way we want to, and we're using condoms, so nothing bad can happen. You can be cool like us too. Just be safe and you won't be sorry!'"

Jim asked Stephen to write down the name of the film, the date it was shown at his school, and the name of the teacher who

82

hosted the assembly. That afternoon he drove over to see Pastor Dixon.

"I hate to get involved in stuff like this," Jim shook his head sadly, "but do you realize what could have happened to Stephen if he'd seen that movie six months ago? Now he knows better. But what about the other kids that don't? I don't think it's right for the school to be showing that kind of thing."

"Jim, you're right. I don't like getting into these things either. But if we don't complain, who will? Maybe a handful of parents. But if a few churches take a stand together, we've got a chance of making a difference. Let's call a few people and see if we can get a group of Christian leaders over to the high school to talk to the principal. Maybe he'll listen. If not, we'll pay the superintendent a visit. He's a good Catholic man, and I have a feeling he wouldn't like that movie any better than we do."

A woman in Pastor Tim's congregation informed him that she had overheard two teenagers from his youth group talking about homosexuality. "I heard every word they said and, believe me, they are involved!" she announced authoritatively.

Pastor Tim felt as if the world had collapsed around him. He decided to confront the two boys, but before doing so, he prayed for wisdom.

"Guys, I need to talk to you about something that was reported to me. A member of the church heard you talking as if you were involved in homosexual behavior. What can you tell me about this? Can you enlighten me a little?"

Gary looked Pastor Tim directly in the eyes and said, "Thank you for not accusing me. Thank you for giving me the benefit of the doubt. It is true that I've been struggling with this issue for awhile, and yes, Phil and I were discussing it one day. But we are not involved with each other, and we aren't going to be."

In the years that followed, both Gary and Phil got married to Christian wives and have been happily married for more than a decade; both couples have children, and both have chosen professions in Christian service. One is overseas in a hostile country; the other in the states with a youth ministry.

Fighting the Good Fight

Is it possible for us to love people and, at the same time, to hate what they are trying to do in our world? One of the most difficult aspects of our Christian response to homosexuality is our eventual encounter with "gay rights" groups and our appropriate response to them. Some of the homosexual advocacy groups operate quietly within the legal system; some write academic papers or teach seminars; some take to the streets, garishly attired and shouting obscenities. Unfortunately, one of their primary targets is the Christian community. More unfortunately, some Christians have chosen to "fight fire with fire," trying to match their rage with "righteous indignation." The results are not good. As James wrote, "My dear brothers, take note of this: Everyone should be quick to listen, slow to speak and slow to become angry, for man's anger does not bring about the righteous life that God desires" (James 1:19).

If rage is not our best weapon, what can we do? Those who have fought on this particular battlefield have some valuable and practical principles that the rest of us can certainly use. Here are some strategies that can make a difference in your community. Perhaps the most important rule of thumb is simply this: *Be Informed.*

1. Do you know what your child is studying? Laws vary from state to state, but according to federal legislation,

every parent has access to all curriculum which is used in public schools and has the legal right to review this material.

2. Are you involved in your child's classroom activities? Teachers welcome volunteers, and Christian parents should be the first to involve themselves in public school classrooms. This, by the way, doesn't mean that we should adopt the role of "enforcers," or go into the school with an attitude of "it's me against them." If we do, teachers will sense it very quickly. Instead, our role should be that of a servant, one who is willing to do whatever is necessary to assist, facilitate, and make life easier for the teacher. If, in the process, we encounter something about which we are concerned regarding sexual education or some other issue, we should lovingly and humbly ask the teacher to explain it to us so we better understand it. Please do not threaten, show indignation, or overreact. An angry approach changes the argument from the issue to a personal confrontation, and it thereby loses its impact.

3. Have you considered having a role on the school board, on an education committee, or in some other leadership capacity? If Christians aren't represented in these areas, people with other agendas, some of them non-Christian or anti-Christian, will be able to make their voices heard without dissent and will thus exert influences in the educational community that might otherwise have been countered.

4. Are you aware of the outside speakers who are visiting your child's school? If a speaker is coming, ask to see an outline of his or her presentation. What has this person written; can you be provided with copies? If you find that

someone with a questionable program is coming to the
school, find out who approved their visit, and be present
at the assembly or classroom presentation. If you have
a disagreement, present it respectfully and without mal-
ice or threat.

5. There is an order of protocol in school organizational
   structures. If there is a problem, discuss it patiently and
   graciously with the appropriate teacher. If this proves to
   be fruitless, then you will need to take the issue to the
   next level—the principal. If the principal is unrespon-
   sive, speak to the superintendent, and then, if necessary,
   bring it before the school board. At every level, please
   show respect for each person by limiting your communication to reasonable and rational dialogue. An angry
   approach and an ugly spirit are counterproductive, not
   only to the addressing of specific issues, but to the cause
   of Christ in the world.

Taking Responsibility for Our Actions

One of the arguments often made by homosexual advocacy
groups is that conservative Christians are hypocrites in
pointing an accusing finger at one behavior and ignoring a
dozen others. "Why don't you address the heterosexual
immorality in the church?" says one group. "How can you
call yourselves Christians and refuse to love homosexuals?"
says another. And, finally, "As Jesus said, 'Let him that is
without sin cast the first stone!'"

First of all, many Christians do overlook extramarital sex,
sex between unmarried couples, cohabitation, and pornography as if they were insignificant. The same person who
refuses to take a strong stand on these matters may be a

hard-liner when faced with a person who exhibits homosexual tendencies, mannerisms, behaviors, or lifestyle choices. In fact, the Scripture is just as clear about heterosexual immorality as it is about homosexuality. Every sexual act that violates scriptural admonitions amounts to an infraction of God's perfect intentions. In short, it is a sin.

Secondly, there is no question about the lack of love some Bible-believing churches demonstrate toward those who are confused about their gender identity. At seminars, like Joe Dallas' "A Christian Response to Homosexuality" workshop, anecdotes abound about the verbal abuse and painful rejection experienced by homosexually-oriented individuals who have sought Christian help. Some of these stories have tragic endings involving self-mutilation or even suicide.[3] It bears repeating that an unloving attitude is just as offensive to God as a sexual sin.

Thirdly, the use of epithets, popular put-downs, and name-calling does not represent the behavior of Jesus Christ. Recently, a well-known Christian television pastor referred to lesbian actress Ellen Degeneres as "Ellen Degenerate" on his broadcast. Such flippancy enlarges an already enormous gulf between Christians and non-Christians, and most specifically between Christians and homosexuals. Why would anyone seek help from an antagonistic foe who mocks, labels, and accuses?

Finally, Jesus did say, "Let him who is without sin cast the first stone," but he was reminding us that we are not to judge. In fact, although he was without sin, he did not pass judgment on repentant sinners. *He did, however, tell the woman taken in adultery, to whom he was speaking, to "go and sin no more."* Or, as we might have said, "Cut it out." In John 3, he told Nicodemus, "For God did not send his Son into the world to condemn the world, but to save the world through him" (v. 17).

Jesus had a far different purpose than that of condemnation. He knew that if penitent women and men came to him, even in the midst of their sin, they could be transformed into new people through spiritual rebirth. Only as we are reborn *from within* can our outward behavior be truly changed. We can only be reborn from within through the touch of Jesus Christ. And we can only be touched by him if we are able to get close to him.

So is it our role, as modern-day disciples, to bring people close enough to Jesus to touch him or to keep them away from him?

Shall we be like the disciples who unsuccessfully tried to hinder the little children from coming to Jesus?[4] As good as their intentions may have been, they completely misunderstood Jesus' priorities and turned out to be a hindrance instead of a help.

Or shall we be identified with the Pharisees—Jesus' least favorite group—who tried to keep a "sinful" woman away from him? Perhaps a review of that ancient story will provide us with a sobering look at what Jesus would do—what Jesus *does* do—when needy sinners try to touch him.

When the Pharisee who had invited him saw this, he said to himself, "If this man were a prophet, he would know who is touching him and what kind of woman she is—that she is a sinner."

Jesus answered him, "Simon, I have something to tell you."

"Tell me, teacher," he said.

"Two men owed money to a certain moneylender. One owed him five hundred denarii, and the other fifty. Neither of them had the money to pay him back, so he canceled the debts of both. Now which of them will love him more?"

Simon replied, "I suppose the one who had the bigger debt canceled."

"You have judged correctly," Jesus said.

Then he turned toward the woman and said to Simon, "Do you see this woman? I came into your house. You did not give me any water for my feet, but she wet my feet with her tears and wiped them with her hair. You did not give me a kiss, but this woman, from the time I entered, has not stopped kissing my feet. You did not put oil on my head, but she has poured perfume on my feet.

"Therefore, I tell you, her many sins have been forgiven— for she loved much. But he who has been forgiven little loves little."

Then Jesus said to her, "Your sins are forgiven."

The other guests began to say among themselves, "Who is this who even forgives sins?"

Jesus said to the woman, "Your faith has saved you; go in peace."[5]

Chapter Five

This Is the Life—Or Is It?

Robert sat in his pastor's office and did his best to look confident and self-assured. He had known Rev. Wilson for most of his life, but rather than making him feel at ease, Robert couldn't help but think that his lifelong friendship with the older man was making matters worse.

"Look, Pastor, I know how you feel about this subject. You think homosexuality is sin, and you have the right to your opinion. But don't you think it's better for me to just come out of hiding and face who I am? If there's anything you don't believe in, it's hypocrisy. You've always made that clear. And I respect you for it."

"That's true, Robert. I hate hypocrisy. But it would be the worst kind of hypocrisy for me to pretend that I'm happy or even at peace with your situation. I know that you're experiencing some confusion about your sexuality, and I'm more than willing to do whatever I can to find some help for you. But I can't just smile and say, 'Oh, that's wonderful!' when you tell me you want

to move to the West Coast and involve yourself in the homosexual community there."

"But you don't understand how alone I feel. No one really
knows me here. No one knows the real me, anyway. The gay
community in L.A. is made of men and women who have faced
the same struggles I've been through. They're my peers, and I
don't have any peers in this town. I don't fit in, no matter how
much I pretend to. Besides," Robert's voice softened, "my friend
Michael is out there, and he's got some work in films lined up
for me. And of course I want to be with him."

Rev. Wilson was not particularly well-informed about the
homosexual lifestyle. He had always found the subject personally
distasteful, so he hadn't made much of an effort to acquaint
himself with information that might have been helpful to
Robert. But he did know one thing, and he was quick to point
it out, "Robert, if you get involved in that way of life, you will
lose so many friends and relatives. You'll even lose whatever
closeness you have with your family, and before long, I'm afraid
you'll find yourself extremely depressed and alienated. Right or
wrong, most small-town folks don't know how to cope with that
kind of thing, and that would include your mom and stepfather.
Have you talked to them about this?"

Robert squirmed in his chair and ran his fingers through his
hair nervously. "Not really . . . not yet. I wouldn't have talked to
you either, if you hadn't asked me about my plans for the coming
year. It just sort of spilled out, and I'm kind of sorry it did."

Rev. Wilson studied young Robert's face with kind, loving
eyes. He'd watched years before as Robert's family was torn
apart by divorce. He'd been brought in more than once to talk to
the boy after difficulties in school had caused him to behave
erratically, and on two occasions, to run away. Wilson had tried
to modify the mother's controlling, impossible-to-please parent-

ing style, and now he was faced with the meticulously groomed, exceptionally handsome, and very determined young man who sat across from him. Robert really did look like a movie star, and considering all, it was a small wonder he hadn't left home and headed for Hollywood a long time before.

"I know you're more than happy to leave your parents. But have you thought about your sisters? Your Grandma? What about the people you hang out with here in town? You're a very popular young man."

"I'm a fraud. They don't even know I'm gay. I've been in the closet long enough, and it's time for me to get real. Reverend, I appreciate your concerns, but the gay lifestyle is nothing terrible—it's simply an alternative. And I happen to think it's the right alternative for me."

L IKE A GLAMOROUS, ALLURING MAGNET, the homosexual community powerfully attracts young men and women who struggle with gender identity. It is particularly desirable to those who are involved in homosexual practices or are emotionally involved with someone of the same sex. But even the curious and the confused who are moving toward the homosexual condition are seduced by the gay lifestyle and all it represents.

I Just Want to Belong

One of the primary reasons for this attraction is that many young people hunger for a place of belonging. As we've seen in previous chapters, social ostracization is one of the most common elements in the development of gender confusion. And once the adolescent begins to wrestle with same-sex emotional attractions and sexual desires, a number of intense and uncomfortable emotions begin to arise. Bud Searcy of Exodus International describes five cycles that frequently affect the lives of these teens:

Cycle of Rejection
Rejection is at the heart of the homosexual struggle.

Cycle of Shame
Shame is close to self-rejection. It does not involve what a person does, but who the person is.

Cycle of Self-Pity
While all of us feel sorry for ourselves from time to time, many homosexuals are locked into a habitual and chronic self-pity cycle.

Cycle of Fear
In their teenage years, many individuals who eventually enter homosexuality seem bound by abnormal levels of fear.

Cycle of Envy
Admiration towards certain types of people soon turns to envy for teens contending with homosexual feelings.[1]

Because of these intense emotional battles, those who face them often feel removed from "normal" people. They describe themselves as being "on the outside looking in." In light of these perceptions, what could be more wonderful than a community of like-minded fellow-strugglers? What could be better than fitting in and feeling at home? What could be more exciting than freedom—total freedom—from judgmental people, religious rules, and cultural taboos?

We live in a very safety conscious society, one that seeks to protect women, men, children, and even animals from every imaginable emotional or physical harm. In recent decades, we have seen cigarette smoking change in the world's eyes from a glamorous style to a foolish and deadly addiction. We've learned to fasten seatbelts in cars and received traffic citations when we didn't. We've managed to get our kids to wear helmets on bikes and motorcycles. We've cut down on our fat intake and increased the roughage in our diets—whether we liked it or not. We've learned to recognize the symptoms of spousal, child, and pet abuse and found out how to report them to authorities.

Perhaps it's time now that we took a long, hard look at the homosexual lifestyle. Maybe we need to assess it with the same level of concern and compassion that found danger in other supposed "freedoms," and made them either unpopular or illegal.

A POPULAR MYTH: Homosexual behavior is an alternative lifestyle—a good, healthy choice for some people.

Consider this: Homosexual behavior is life threatening. A journal report in the October 1996 *Princeton Theological Review* indicates that the physical dangers involved in homosexuality make it a high-risk lifestyle choice. HIV and AIDS, of course, speak for themselves as a life-and-death peril. But other threats, including much higher murder and suicide rates, dangers from hepatitis B, syphilis, herpes, and "a host of other blood-borne diseases" also threaten lives. This is, in large part, due to the promiscuity which is prevalent in the homosexual community. A survey by the American Psychological Association reported that the average homosexual has 50 partners a year. George Rekers has stated that one 18-year-old homosexual reported having had 3,000 sexual partners.

Some studies indicate that the average life span is dramatically shorter for a male homosexual; others reflect that less than 3 percent of all homosexuals surveyed are over the age of 55. If we are concerned about the dangers of smoking, drug and alcohol abuse, we should also be concerned about the death risks inherent in homosexual behavior.

What Have I Got to Lose?

"I've got to get out of the house! I can't stand another day with my father, and my mother doesn't even see him for what he really is . . ."

"I want to be with my partner. We want to live together and share our lives. We're tired of sneaking around."

"There's this hunger in me for more excitement, more thrills, more experiences. I'll never be able to satisfy it in this disgusting little town."

"I want to go live where I belong, and that's among the people who are like me—other homosexuals. I know that once I'm with them, I'll have found my place in the world."

These statements reflect more than a whim or a passing fancy. They express the heart's cry of many of those who have same-sex attractions. These disenfranchised individuals feel that they are trapped in some sort of an emotional no man's land, and they long to be settled and safe. And, of

course, the unkindness and lack of acceptance they sometimes experience drives them, in their deep loneliness and
sense of alienation, away from the very people who might
provide the love they so deeply desire.

As appealing as the homosexual lifestyle seems to those
who are in search of a more rewarding emotional environment, some warning flags need to be raised. The first red flag
should fly in the face of those who refuse to reach out in love
to those who struggle with gender identity. Our lack of sensitivity, grace, and Christian understanding contribute to the
relentless magnetism of the gay community.

Unfortunately, that community is not the haven of
healthy, happy, and honest interaction that it claims to be.
There are important warning flags to be heeded there too—
three specific areas of risk that must not be overlooked in the
homosexual lifestyle are: emotional risks, physical risks, and
spiritual risks.

The emotional crises faced by young people who, like
Robert, pack up, leave home, and seek shelter in the gay
community are acute and painful. They are vividly described
in a book written to help homosexual activists bring young
people "out," a process that they view as a rite of passage.
Here's how the authors describe the traumatic, lifetime
losses "coming out" usually causes:

> In the minds of some youth, giving up heterosexual roles
> and institutions is more than a "sexual" matter; it is a loss of
> cultural identity, a break with historical tradition. The Asian
> who finds that he will not be able to carry on the family and
> clan tradition, the black who may no longer attend the neigh-
> borhood church, the Italian-American who is rejected by his
> parents and can no longer attend extended family functions—

these are soul-wrenching losses of such an immense magnitude that they signify the loss of a whole way of life. To lose all of this in order to gain the public expression of sexual desires may seem like a bad trade-off. Some adults can handle the anxiety created by this declaration, but for many youth it is too much to bear.[2]

This is a sobering evaluation from the homosexual community itself. But it may not go far enough. Countless people within the gay community are faced with enormous emotional challenges. There are many reasons for this. For one thing, as we've seen before, a difficult family background is clearly a factor in the choice of homosexual behavior. Social rejection and past abuse or sexual molestation may have contributed to the decision. Intense emotional attachments and powerful sexual encounters, losses of friends and family, and health fears all complicate the emotional disarray that is often found among active homosexuals.

Marshall Kirk and Hunter Madsen, in their book *After the Ball: How America Will Conquer Its Fear and Hatred of Gays in the '90s* write, "Now the most distressing thing about this American myth of the unhappy homosexual is that it does have some basis in fact. Studies suggest that, while most gays are remarkably well adjusted in light of their stigma, on the whole, gay men (and to a lesser extent lesbians) are more prone to feelings of loneliness, anxiety, paranoia, depression and unhappiness than are straights. (Moreover, the often-unpleasant quality of social life among gays themselves is, to a considerable degree, the result of these individual maladjustments.)"[3]

Drug and alcohol abuse rates are much higher in the homosexual community. Gay men abuse alcohol at least twice as often as males in general[4] and lesbians have a seven times higher rate of alcoholism than women in general.[5] One study of gay and bisexual male adolescents reports that lifetime use of alcohol was 76 percent among those surveyed, marijuana 42 percent, and cocaine/crack 25 percent.[6]

Many studies indicate that suicide is much more common in the homosexual community than in the heterosexual community.

- In a study of gay and bisexual male adolescents, 30 percent attempted suicide at least once.

- In a study of 5,000 gay men and women, 35 percent of gay men and 38 percent of gay women had seriously considered or attempted suicide.[7]

- In a national survey of lesbians, 24 percent between 17 and 24 years old attempted suicide, and 32 percent had thoughts of suicide.[8]

Whatever the emotional problems faced by gender-confused men and women, moving into the homosexual community does not solve them. And emotional dangers—most notably depression, even to the point of suicide—are not the only risks faced by those who seek solace and belonging in the gay lifestyle.

What Could I Have Done?

Ever since he'd noticed that his secretary had penciled it on his calendar, Rev. Wilson had been dreading the appointment with Robert's mother. She was, to say the least, not exactly his favorite church member. But now, as she walked into his office, her usual arrogance and condescension were nowhere to be seen.

Instead her distress was almost palpable, hanging in the air like a mist of pain.

"Pastor," she began, even before she seated herself, "have you heard about Robert?"

He looked at her face and quickly determined that she was dealing with more than her usual disapproval and control. "About Robert? Has something happened to him?"

"Well, you know that he's living in L.A. with his, you know . . . his friend Michael, right?"

"Yes, I know about that. He talked to me about it before he left. I tried to discourage him, but his mind was made up. He's been there for nearly a year, hasn't he?"

"A year next week. But that's not what I meant. Have you heard about his test results?"

Rev. Wilson looked puzzled, trying to remember what Robert had told him. "Test? You mean a screen test? What kind of test?"

"A blood test. He's HIV positive."

He sucked in his breath as if he had received a physical blow, and tears stung his eyes, "Oh, Lord, no. I'm so sorry. I had no idea."

"I thought he might have called you. He was, of course, terribly depressed. Apparently Michael never bothered to tell him that he was positive, and, well, they weren't careful . . ." Her voice broke, and she begin to cry. "I hate talking about this—it's so . . . so . . . terrible for all of us."

"Would it be all right if I called Robert? Does he know that you're talking to me?"

Anger flashed in her eyes, "What difference does it make what he thinks? He's brought it on himself—no, he's brought it on all of us. What am I supposed to tell my friends? How can I explain this?"

Rev. Wilson fought off his own anger, and he kept his voice as calm as possible. "I can understand your feelings, but right at the moment. my greatest concern is for Robert. I'd like for you to tell him you've talked to me and that I would very much like to speak with him. He's dear to my heart, and he needs some support right now. Once I've talked to him, we can talk about your situation, if you wish. But let's focus on Robert for now."

After Robert's mother left the office, Rev. Wilson sat for several minutes with his face in his hands, feeling both weary and grieved. What could he have done differently? What should he have said? Would anything have made any difference in Robert's decision?

With a heavy sigh, he stood up, stared out the window for a moment and paged his secretary on the intercom, "I'm going for a little walk," he explained. "I need some fresh air." With a heavy heart, he stepped out into the cold fall air, wishing with all his heart that he could have made a greater difference in Robert's life. "God help me," he prayed quietly. "But what could I have done?"

Health risks for homosexuals, particularly for males, are not limited to AIDS, but AIDS is, at least for now, the most visible and deadly threat. A homosexual author laments, "Who wants to encourage their kids to engage in a life that exposes them to a 50 percent chance of HIV infection? Who even wants to be neutral about such a possibility? If the rationale behind social toleration of homosexuality is that it allows gay kids an equal shot at the pursuit of happiness, that rationale is hopelessly undermined by an endless epidemic that negates happiness."[9]

It is clear that inappropriate sexual activity of any kind leads to various kinds of sexually transmitted diseases (STDs), and it only takes one exposure to these bacteria and

viruses for them to be transmitted. Heterosexual promiscuity also creates major health risks and can communicate
such viruses as genital herpes, genital warts, and even
HIV (not to mention the matter of unplanned pregnancy).
But the statistics on HIV indicate that it is primarily transmitted by men having sex with men. In a 1994–1995
American survey, males who have sex with males
accounted for 51 percent of all AIDS victims, contrasted
with 8 percent among those who reported only heterosexual contact.[10]

*The results of scientific studies on sexual behavior clearly
favor the Christian conservative in the public forum. But
where is the voice that focuses public attention on these
findings? Our society still regards scientific research as
authoritative, and with the tide of evidence heavily in our
favor, we can state convincingly that there are compelling
and rational reasons for not promoting the gay lifestyle in
any form. —Matthew Frawley[11]*

The argument is made that if homosexuals remained
monogamous, or if they practiced only safe sex, the threat
of AIDS would be dramatically reduced. Both statements
are true. But they are not noted for lifelong relationships,
even though a few claim to have a monogamous relationship. Statistics on the number of partners varies, but it
is estimated that some homosexual males have sex with as
many as 500 partners in a lifetime. That figure may be debat-
able, but Michael Warner, an English professor at Rutgers
University, argues that promiscuous sex is the "essence of
gay liberation." A news story explains, "While it may be difficult for heterosexuals to understand anonymous sex with

multiple partners, to many homosexuals it is a cornerstone of liberation."[12] For Warner and others, promiscuity is part of what it means to be gay.

Along similar lines, homosexuals are rejecting the idea of "safe-sex" because it inhibits the pleasures that they see as part of their identity. There has been much discussion and speculation about the reasons for it, such as nihilism, the belief that a cure for AIDS is about to be revealed, and self-destructive psychological patterns. Whatever the reasons, from a 1997 survey of 205 gay men in Miami's South Beach, Dr. William W. Darrow, a public health professor, found that 45 percent had unprotected anal sex in the past year.[13] Similar results have been cited in other reports.

The risks of AIDS are inarguable, and despite the millions of dollars poured into research, the news is not encouraging. As Gabriel Rotello writes in *The Advocate*, a popular homosexual magazine, "There's no way a 15-year-old can say to himself that AIDS isn't real, that it's just some homophobic stereotype, a lie designed to make queers look bad. AIDS is as real as it gets, and any bright kid digging through the library is going to find little solace in statistics predicting that a third of gay males of his generation will be HIV-infected by age 30, half by age 50."[14]

Of course AIDS is not the only health threat faced by the homosexual community. The prestigious *Journal of the American Medical Association*, in a Council Report to physicians, makes the following points:

- There is an 84-to-1 relative risk of anal cancer after AIDS diagnosis among gay men compared with the incidence of anal carcinoma in age-matched and sex-matched persons in the general population.

- Most cases of anal syphilis occur in gay men.

- Gay men are at increased risk for a number of gastrointestinal infections and STDs.

- Lesbians who are at risk for certain cancers and other risk factors are sometimes poorly diagnosed because they do not reveal their sexual orientation.[15]

Other reports on health risks among homosexuals concur:

- Three-quarters of male homosexuals will acquire an STD in a lifetime, and well over a third will do so in any one year.[16]

- The overall life expectancy of male homosexuals is around thirty years less than their straight counterparts.[17]

When young people who are drawn toward homosexual behavior feel isolated, rejected, and abandoned, they are enchanted by the fantasy that they will be loved and welcomed into the homosexual community. They may, indeed, find a group of peers that have experienced similar feelings and desires. But the sense of being "home at last" is deceptive. If it is home, it is no safer than the troubled home they left behind. And if life there didn't seem worth living, another question arises: *is the homosexual lifestyle worth dying for?*

Is It Too Late to Go Home?

Besides the emotional and physical dangers, there are also spiritual risks involved in the homosexual lifestyle. For young people who have grown up in a Christian environment, for those who have experienced a relationship with Jesus Christ, or for those who have participated in Christianity, there is spiritual turmoil. There is fear in some that they have been abandoned by God, or that they have committed the "unpardonable sin." During the times when they've needed God the most, these men and women have felt the most cut off and the least able to reach out and receive the love and compassion of God they once knew. And those who have never received Jesus Christ into their lives are even more at risk.

When Rev. Wilson saw Robert sitting in his office, for a couple of seconds he didn't recognize him. The handsome young man was astonishingly thin, and his skin had the pallor of ill health. But worst of all, at least for his pastor, was the lonely, haunted look in his eyes. It was an encounter the pastor would never forget, made worse by the fact that he simply did not know what to say. He was at a such a loss for words that Robert finally broke the silence for him.

"Pastor, I hope you're not going to say 'I told you so.'"

Rev. Wilson shook his head sadly. "I wish that were possible— I wish I had told you something—anything—to try and change your mind about moving west. The truth is, I didn't tell you much of anything."

"Don't blame yourself, Rev. Wilson. It was my decision, not yours."

"I know that. But Robert, this is such a difficult time. It's terrible. I wish there were something I could do to help you. What can I do? What can the church do? Do you need any particular kind of treatment?"

"I'm as good as lost, Pastor. There's no hope for me now." Robert's voice wasn't so much self-pitying as matter-of-fact. "If a

person has big bucks, he can fight this disease and at least buy some time. But that's not the way it is for me."

"How much money?"

Robert chuckled, "More than you or I will ever see, believe me."

Rev. Wilson shook his head sadly. "I'm just glad you came home, Robert. Your mother seems to have worked through most of her anger, and I think she'll be very kind to you."

Robert nodded and managed a crooked little smile. "She actually apologized to me for being angry at me. It's a strange situation, having a disease like this. It must be a little like being a smoker who gets lung cancer. Half of the people you know blame you for being sick. A lot of people aren't really that sympathetic, because they figure if you're gay, you've got it coming."

"Robert, I hope you don't think any of us feel that way. If I blame anyone, I blame myself. I wish I'd known more about the risks you were facing before you left here. And I wish I'd known more about the prevention of homosexuality. Maybe all this could have been avoided if I'd kept myself in touch with what's happening. Maybe we could have helped you."

"Pastor, I can remember a time, when I was in junior high, when I might have been open to some sort of prevention, or intervention, or whatever. Back then, even though I felt some attraction to other boys, I didn't want to be a homosexual. I hated it when the others called me a 'faggot,' and I used to dream about getting a girlfriend just to prove them wrong. But by the time I came in here and told you about Michael and about moving to L.A., I'd already become sexually active. I was emotionally involved with Michael by then, and I don't think I would have heard you, no matter what you'd said. By then, I was convinced that I was gay, and that there was no other lifestyle for me."

"What do you think now?"

"There's so much I don't understand. But I know one thing— barring some kind of a miracle, I'm going to die of this thing before too long. And I want to get myself back in touch with God now. Not just because I'm worried about heaven, either. Over these past few years, I've felt so distant from God, so cut off from his love. I've missed you, my church friends, the music, even the Bible. For a long time, I couldn't even stand to see a Bible in the room, and I put it out of sight. Now I feel hungry to read it. I guess I'm like the prodigal son, and I've finally found my way back home. Trouble is, I got home a little too late to save my life."

In some ways, our walk with God seems fragile. Because we are emotional people, our "feelings" about God change as quickly as the weather, and we don't always feel "in touch" with him. Every Christian goes through times when God seems distant, when the heavens seem like brass, when life in the Spirit seems like a mind game. During those times, we are often driven to our knees and to our Bibles. We may rail at God, we may be angry about his "silence" and alleged inactivity, but we rarely stop thinking about our need for him.

When we are involved in ongoing sin, the equation changes somewhat. We are not only emotionally removed from our walk with God, we are secretly afraid that it can never again be recovered. We recall the many scriptures that talk about God's anger, God's judgment, and the fact that sin separates humans from God, and we wonder in our hearts whether God still cares about us. In times like these, other spiritual voices join the accusations of our own conscience and remind us incessantly of our failures, our weaknesses, and our unrighteousness. We become discouraged, fearful, and sometimes rebellious that God's rules don't make room for our carnal desires.

Worse yet, when our sin is something to which we are emotionally attached, we find it impossible to repent. People with addictions know all too well the pattern of shame and sorrow that makes them long for God's healing, but instead sends them rushing right back into their addictive behavior. In the case of people who are carrying on heterosexual affairs, powerful emotional and sexual attractions cause them to feel as if they cannot give up the "one thing that matters." They cling to ideas like the song lyric that says, "It can't be wrong if it feels so right." And they try to ignore the damage that is done to their spirits.

In the case of homosexuality, the person simply cannot believe in repentance, because repentance demands change, and change, for someone involved in homosexual behavior, seems absolutely impossible. In actual fact, sin is sin. And no matter what our weakness may be—anger, lust, greed, jealousy, laziness, hatred—we all find ourselves saying the same kinds of things, consciously or unconsciously:

"I can't help it! It's just the way I am."

"God made me like this—he'll just have to live with it."

"I'd change if I could, but I can't so I won't."

The apostle Paul, when faced with his own sinful nature, expressed the dilemma eloquently: "So I find this law at work: When I want to do good, evil is right there with me. For in my inner being I delight in God's law; but I see another law at work in the members of my body, waging war against the law of my mind and making me a prisoner of the law of sin at work within my members. What a wretched man I am! Who will rescue me from this body of death?" (Romans 7:21–24).

Paul goes on to write one of the most welcome messages

ever written to sinners: "Therefore, there is now no condemnation for those who are in Christ Jesus, because through Christ Jesus the law of the Spirit of life set me free from the law of sin and death" (Romans 8:1–2).

Does this mean, then, that we needn't repent, because the price has been paid for our sins, and we don't need to worry about our shortcomings? No, but it means that through Christ we are able to receive salvation even in the midst of our struggle with sin. However, throughout the New Testament, from the message of John the Baptist as he prepared the way for Jesus through the letters to the churches in the book of Revelation, repentance from sin has always preceded a relationship with Jesus Christ. Even if we have already invited him into our lives, we still have to repent in order to be in fellowship with him. In short, we can't continue in sin and walk with him as if nothing were wrong.

First John 1:9 says, "If we confess our sins, he is faithful and just and will forgive us our sins and purify us from all unrighteousness." The verse starts with the little word *if*, and the implication of that word is that if we *don't* confess, he won't be able to forgive and cleanse us.

What does all this have to do with the risks involved in the homosexual lifestyle? The gay community, as a whole, does not believe that homosexuality is sin. Those who have chosen homosexuality as an identity believe that they have done the right thing, not the wrong thing. And within that gay community, any talk of repentance or sin will be discredited, mocked, or angrily rejected. Even the self-described Christian churches in the community reinterpret Scripture, as we learned in the last chapter, to remove all negative statements about homosexuality.

The homosexual lifestyle is a field replete with emotional

land mines, and few are untouched by its pain, confusion, and upheaval. It is a war zone that threatens those who live there with disease, drugs, depression, and death. Perhaps worst of all, from an eternal perspective, it is a place where a personal relationship with the God of the Bible is unlikely to be sustained and where the loss of his presence is felt often and acutely by those who have once walked with him. Suffice it to say that ongoing, unrepentant sin means, at the very least, that our relationship with God is damaged and we are left to struggle with the consequences of our behavior without his close friendship and constant guidance.

A friend of mine, who left the homosexual community after more than twenty-five years of involvement, says that the worst aspect of the entire experience was the unbridled self-absorption of the culture: "The greatest danger, in my view—and it is a great spiritual danger—is the intense narcissism in the gay community. The consequence of this narcissism is a complete absence of intimacy. This may seem contradictory, considering the myriad sexual intimacies that take place. But true Christian intimacy, which is the capacity to deeply, compassionately and empathetically know other human beings and be known by them, is impossible in a world where narcissism is rampant."[18]

To turn from such a way of life requires the transformation of one's thought patterns, conditioned responses, and habits of behavior. It is, without question, a daunting choice, much like turning from lifelong idolatry to faith in the true God. If the choice is made in faith, it requires the casting of one's future into the wind of God's Spirit and leaving all the many possible results in Christ's hands.

And what can be expected of God when a sinner who longs to get back to him determines that it's time to repent and head for home? For that matter, what can we expect of faithful Christians who watch that sinner return weak, wounded, and worse for the wear? Fortunately, there is a prototype that helps us know what to expect from God and what God expects from us.

Jesus told the story about one particular young man who decided that he'd had enough of life in the fast lane. After suffering deprivation, loneliness, and sickness, he decided to go back to his father, no matter what. We don't know what kind of sin he got involved in while he was engaged in a different lifestyle. We don't know specifically what he did, or why, or with whom, but we are told that he wasted all his money on what Jesus called "wild living." Finally, he turned his eyes homeward.

> When he came to his senses, . . . he got up and went to his father.
> But while he was still a long way off, his father saw him and was filled with compassion for him; he ran to his son, threw his arms around him and kissed him.
> The son said to him, "Father, I have sinned against heaven and against you. I am no longer worthy to be called your son."
> But the father said to his servants, "Quick! Bring the best robe and put it on him. Put a ring on his finger and sandals on his feet. Bring the fattened calf and kill it. Let's have a feast and celebrate. For this son of mine was dead and is alive again; he was lost and is found." So they began to celebrate.
> Meanwhile, the older son was in the field. When he came near the house, he heard music and dancing. So he called one of the servants and asked him what was going on. "Your brother has come," he replied, "and your father has killed the fattened calf because he has him back safe and sound."

The older brother became angry and refused to go in. So his father went out and pleaded with him. But he answered his father, "Look! All these years I've been slaving for you and never disobeyed your orders. Yet you never gave me even a young goat so I could celebrate with my friends. But when this son of yours who has squandered your property with prostitutes comes home, you kill the fattened calf for him!"

"My son," the father said, "you are always with me, and everything I have is yours. But we had to celebrate and be glad, because this brother of yours was dead and is alive again; he was lost and is found."[19]

Part Two:

Relating & Relationships

So far we have explored and explained some of the issues that surround homosexuality. We've considered childhood experiences, cultural mores, Christian attitudes, and all the variables that set the stage for a homosexual orientation in men and women. And we've tried to concentrate on how we can help prevent young people from choosing to pursue behavior that may eventually lead to a homosexual lifestyle.

Now I would like to shift the format a little. For the next couple of chapters, I invite you to join me and my friend Sam in my living room. It's cold outside and we are sitting comfortably, sipping some hot coffee in front of a crackling fireplace.

Sam called me to set up the meeting. He wanted to chat—he said something about his family falling apart. "And, to top it all off," he said, "I think one of my sons may be a homosexual."

Sam knew that I'd been involved with some people with AIDS and with those having family problems. "And I hear you're trying to do something about the prevention of homosexuality," he added.

Sam and I had been fishing partners for years, and like many men, we'd never really discussed our personal lives. But suddenly, Sam felt a need to talk to me about some very personal, very difficult issues. You'll notice that at first, we won't be talking about homosexuality at all. Instead, we'll be discussing the family and the home environment. You may hear me say some things I've said before if I think something I've already covered in part 1 is worth repeating. At the very end, we'll talk about what may be the most important aspect of all—forgiveness—because, as you know by now, the problem of same-sex attraction begins with hurtful relationships and the damage they do. If those of us who are actively involved in such situations are wise and godly, perhaps that can also be where it ends.

Chapter Six

How Can We Create a Loving Home?

My friend Sam and I settled down in our chairs, facing the fire-place. We made small talk for a while, and then I tried to steer the conversation toward Sam's concerns. "Well, Sam, before we get started, I want to make sure that you understand a couple of things. First of all there's a basic difference between you and me. Do you have any idea what that is?"

Sam stared at me for a second or two, and then he chuckled, "Yeah, Don. You've got gray hair so I guess you're somewhat older than I am."

"That's right. I'm a lot older than you. But that's not my point. I want you to know that, in all probability, I've made more mistakes in life than you have. And if you can learn and profit from my mistakes, then we'll make progress."

Sam looked a little surprised. "That's a different angle than I expected from you, Don."

I nodded and continued, "Here's the second point I'd like to make. This comes from my high school class motto: 'Knowledge without application makes but half the man or woman.' Jesus Christ made a similar statement recorded for us in Matthew 7:24–27. He told the story of one man who built his house on sand and another man who built his house on a rock. When rough weather hit, the only house left standing was the one built on rock. Jesus compared building on rock to a wise person who not only hears God's Word, but acts to build his or her life upon it."

Sam looked me in the eye, a very serious expression on his face. "I wouldn't be here if I didn't intend to put your advice into action."

"Well, Sam, you're a wise person if you have a desire to see changes in your own life, and even more so if you want to make life better for those you love."

"Don, the fact is, my life situation can't continue status quo."

I could see from Sam's earnest words and expression that he had come through the door with an open mind and an open heart. My goal was to help him see some of the behavioral patterns that have a tendency to wreck families. By now I'd learned that those same things also set the stage for a young person to be attracted to the homosexual lifestyle. I knew that by helping Sam get his family on more solid ground, I'd be helping his son too.

"Sam, I want to begin by laying down some basic groundwork for healthy family living and communication. These principles hold true for every person—male or female, married or single, parent or childless, young or old. Every normal person experiences three basic needs. And we need them all the time."

Sam nodded eagerly, "You mean things like food, shelter, and warmth, right?"

"Those things are important, but right now we're talking about relationships. I'm referring to a different set of needs.

Emotionally, every person needs three things: we need to be listened to, to feel appreciated, and to be taken seriously."

Sam's face reflected a quick grasp of the three needs, but like most of us, his first response was about himself—yes, of course, that's what he needed. It took a few more minutes of consideration before he was able to extend those needs to the other members of his immediate family. Once he was able to see that, we were on our way to some constructive conversation.

Learning to Listen

As adults, we feel we're receiving a huge compliment when we are really listened to. Having someone's full and undivided attention tells us that we are important to the person we're talking to, and usually we come away with the feeling that we're liked. We have an opposite reaction when a person walks away in the middle of a sentence, leaving us standing with our mouths open. When this occurs, we feel hurt, rejected, and insulted. Most of all, we feel unimportant to them. Nobody likes that feeling.

Some people are better at listening than others. Many of us—and I must include myself—have struggled all our lives to be good listeners. Maybe we're self-centered. Maybe we're afraid someone will make an important point before we do. Or maybe it's simply not part of our personality style to listen to other people's ideas. The fact is, even if we would rather state our case and move on, we should all be in the process of learning to stop and listen.

Early in our marriage, when my wife Diana returned home after a hard day at the office, I learned that if I would just sit down, give her my full attention, and really listen without offering my "brilliant" advice, she would feel free to share her frustrations at work. Once she'd aired her grievances, soon she would be whistling away, doing whatever she had to do with a lighter heart. The key to seeing her enjoy a pleasant evening seemed to require only that I sit down, listen attentively, and keep my mouth shut. What Diana needed was a sounding board; she had a need to feel really heard. In any case, it wasn't a bad idea for me to stop advising her about her work. I really didn't know much about it, anyway.

Naturally, men also have a need to be listened to. A wife can really build up her husband by being genuinely interested in his work or in what he is doing. We males may, however, find it easier to talk about abstract, less personal things than women. The point is this: we all want to be heard. The same need to be listened to exists in both sexes.

The art of listening may seem like a small issue. But it can evolve into a big marital mess when another person who is not a spouse steps in to meet this need. Secretaries, old girlfriends or boyfriends, concerned neighbors, coworkers, friendly acquaintances—all these have the potential of becoming participants in extramarital affairs with lonely husbands or wives. Sinful sexual liaisons often begin with heartfelt conversations, and not necessarily with instantaneous eroticism or unmitigated lust.

Huge problems are also created when children become the ones who have problems dumped on them by parents. Many times, the issues they hear about are beyond their age of maturity. Children who are forced to become confidants to their mothers or fathers stand a good chance of becoming very warped in relating to either or both parents. In fact, this kind of unhealthy interaction can be one factor in the development of homosexual tendencies.

In his article "Healing Homosexuality," Richard Cohen

makes the following statement: "The homosexual love need is essentially a search for parenting. What the homosexual seeks to fulfill are normal needs for bonding that have been abnormally left unmet in the process of growth."[1] Clearly, when a child must serve as a confessor, advisor, or confidant to a parent, he or she is not being parented in a wholesome and constructive way.

> I suggest that the homosexual condition is to be linked—not with genetic predisposition, hormonal imbalance, or even abnormal learning processes as commonly understood—but with difficulties in the parent-child relationship, especially in the early years of life.
> —Elizabeth Moberly[2]

Sam may not have yet learned to listen to his wife, but at the moment, he was listening very carefully to me. I wanted him to say a little more about his situation, so I asked, "Sam, do you think children have the same need of being really listened to as adults?"

"I guess that question has never really crossed my mind, Don. But I suppose their needs would be the same as ours. Come to think of it, I sort of remember feeling that nobody listened to me when I was a child. I was always told, 'Children should be seen, but not heard.' I recall feeling somewhat frustrated in my growing up years, but I couldn't quite figure out why."

Adults are supposed to know better, yet most of us seem to be amazingly skilled at passing along to our children our own negative childhood experiences and destructive family patterns. We do it without giving it a second thought. And the only way the negative cycle ever stops is when we recognize the faults in our own upbringing and make a conscious decision to stop duplicating our parents' mistakes.

The reality is that children have an even greater need to be listened to than adults do. It is very frustrating to them and devastating to their development not to be allowed to participate in significant interaction with their parents. Then, by the time our sons and daughters reach adolescence, they are the ones who short-circuit the communication.

When our boys were teenagers, it seemed as if we could never get them to share what was going on in their lives, no matter how much we tried talking to them. We always got the same answers: "Nothing much," or "I dunno," and off they went. The less they talked to us, the more concerned we became. All our best efforts yielded nothing—we simply could not get them to interact with us on a personal level. Sometimes they would report facts about whatever we asked, but there was no communication from the heart.

One morning we took them out to brunch and, for the first time in years, they started talking about *real* things. We were rather shocked, and we wondered just what had "primed their pump." We discovered two interesting things.

First of all, being in a restaurant meant we had the boys all to ourselves. At home it seemed as if the neighbor kids were always waiting for them with all sorts of things to do. Now we had their undivided attention. Second, the restaurant was neutral turf, while our home was permeated with parental authority. At a restaurant, we were on common ground and the boys were on an even playing field and once we realized what an opportunity it could be, we planned brunch every weekend. It turned out to be a real blessing for all of us.

Jesus was a gifted listener. The New Testament reveals that he not only listened in depth but responded with unique understanding to two very different sisters who were faced with the same problem. Each sister had a unique personality type and therefore a different set of felt needs. In John 11:1–46 we read about the death of Mary and Martha's brother Lazarus. Ultimately, Jesus did the most remarkable thing he could have done for either of them—he raised Lazarus from the dead.

But before the miracle, when approached by Martha who was an analytical type, Jesus met her need by having a meaningful and instructional dialogue with her. Mary, on the other hand was a very sensitive, intuitive person. Jesus met her need without dialogue—he simply wept with her.

As a father and husband, I learn from Jesus' example that I should try to know each person in my family so well that I can respond to their personal needs in a specific and nurturing way. This cannot be done without careful listening on my part.

Not being listened to can become a source of hurt, whether conscious or unconscious, which can erode and damage relationships. It can lead to unhealthy attachments. Being listened to is a very real need, and our ability to meet it will determine to whom or to what behavior our loved ones will turn in order to get their needs met. When our children are not listened to, it can impede their development.

I've enjoyed looking at the life and ministry of Jesus. I get a very different picture from the image so many of us try to wear. Jesus, for instance, seemed to attract children. I've never seen children attracted to a gruff, stern person. They avoid people like that. Children are great judges of

character; they "read" people well and can tell when adults
don't like them. But children flocked to Jesus. To me that
says that Jesus was able to smile, to enjoy life, to have fun
even with children. He was able to be himself. —Jay Kesler[3]

The Fine Art of Giving Appreciation

*As I listened to Sam, he began to talk about a feeling most
spouses have had at one time or another. "I don't know about
you, Don, but I can sure relate to that second need you mentioned—feeling appreciated. Just last night, when I returned
from a hard day at the office, the first thing I was greeted with
was a series of questions. 'Did you deposit your paycheck?' 'Did
you call a repairman? The washing machine is leaking water
all over the floor.' 'Would you drop Judy off at her piano lesson
and pick up some milk on your way home?' All that in the first
ten seconds!"*

*"Maybe, Sam, it's not so much what your wife said. Maybe
it's what she didn't say that left you feeling used," I suggested.*

*"Exactly. She never says she's glad to see me unless she wants
something from me. She never says anything about who I am.
Maybe I'm wrong, but my gut tells me she's only interested in
what I do for her."*

*"So you're a needed item in the function of the household, but
you don't feel appreciated for what you contribute?"*

*"I think you've got the idea, Don—I just feel like a machine
that cranks out the money to keep everybody else happy."*

*"But wait a minute, Sam. Didn't you tell me when we first
met that this 'feeling' business was just a woman's thing? I think
you mentioned that real men don't let their feelings hang out—
they handle every matter that comes along calmly and logically.
Am I right?"*

Sam looked a little uncomfortable. "I'm not so sure I like the tape being played back to me, but yeah, I guess you're right."

"Sorry, Sam, but tell me, do you think your spouse feels appreciated by you?"

"I think so—just last week I told her the meal she fixed tasted pretty good. That's saying that I appreciate what she did for me. She sort of smiled and said thanks. But I try to be conservative about that sort of thing. Compliments should be sincere and special. A man wouldn't want to say too much—his wife might get proud or something like that."

"So you complimented her performance of cooking one good meal that you happened to like, but normally you don't compliment her or show appreciation to her for either what she does or for who she is to you—right? Do you realize you also inferred that all the other meals she cooks for you were not up to your expected standard?"

"So what's the difference? I don't know what you're talking about—you're not making sense, Don!"

"Sam, have you ever just said to your lovely wife, 'Honey, I just love you for being you!'? Have you ever bought her flowers for no special occasion and with no hidden agenda, but just because you wanted to communicate to her how much you cared for her and loved her?"

There was a rather lengthy pause, "Do you do that stuff, Don?"

"Yes, but I wish I could say I do it a lot more than I do. Diana is my very special friend, wife, mother to our boys, and the love of my life."

Sam stared at me. He was struggling with annoyance, but beyond that he was aware that we were getting close to some important problems. Finally, he asked the question that was

stuck in his throat, "Don, do you say those words—you know—
like 'I love you'?"

From the time Diana and I were first married I really,
truly loved her. But verbalizing my feelings in words was one
of the hardest things I'd ever done. I felt very weird and out
of character trying to say loving and gentle things. She often
told me how much she loved me, and you'd think that would
have helped. But the ability to express my love in words was
something I had to learn and develop over many years.

Once again, the source of the problem lay in the skills I
learned growing up in my own family. I knew my parents
loved me, but speaking (or hearing) the phrase "I love you"
was not a common event in those days. Fortunately, although
I was a slow learner, saying "I love you" is now a very natural
part of my verbal expression. Rarely does anyone in our
immediate family end a telephone conversation without saying "I love you." But it was not always that way. And we went
through some very rough waters as a family before things
changed.

Most of us are most comfortable with the same level of
loving expression we experienced in childhood. Unless we
consciously seek to change the patterns we learned from our
parents, we will treat those closest to us the way we were
treated. And many of us never felt appreciated as children.

*"So in everything, do to others what you would have them
do to you, for this sums up the Law and the Prophets."*
(Matthew 7:12)

For example, most of us want our children to excel
beyond our own accomplishments. Having higher standards

and expectations is honorable, but do we compliment our children and do they feel appreciated, whether they meet our standards or not?

There was a time when only rarely would I give my sons what I thought was a compliment for a performance. The rest of the time, at least from my perspective, they just didn't measure up. Our sons were not what you would call "academic" types, and they really had to put in a lot of hours of studying for the grades they received. My fatherly expectations were quite often beyond their level of achievement. In certain subjects they really excelled, which made me proud. But I expected excellence in every area and believed that if they did not do one hundred percent in everything, they did not deserve any compliments from me.

At one son's graduation ceremony from junior high, I watched as students were acknowledged for their various academic achievements. As a variety of scholastic awards were given out, I sat there wishing my kid would get one. I was sort of blaming myself and thinking, *My kids just don't have what it takes.*

At the very end of the ceremony, before the diplomas were handed out, the principal made one more presentation. "We now have a very special award," he explained, "that we have never given out before in this school's history. This is an award for exceptional sportsmanship and conduct, both on the athletic field and in the classroom. This student has also displayed mature character in his relationships with fellow students and teachers. May I present this special award to . . ."

Before I could catch my breath, my son was striding up the aisle to receive this wonderful honor. I quickly realized that if he had won all the other awards and achievements together, it could not have made us prouder. Our son had displayed inner character and sensitivity to his classmates and teachers even when he was away from home, when we weren't there to control him. What more could we have wanted?

Needless to say, I quickly did some soul searching. I couldn't wait to give him a very big hug and to tell him how proud I was—how proud both Diana and I were—of him and of who he was.

That was an important turning point for me, a time when I realized that my sons deserved far more credit than I had been willing to give them. I began to express myself far more generously after that. I thank God that today both of our sons are doing very well in their professions, and we hear very positive comments from their peers and bosses on the quality of work and character they exhibit. I only wish I'd understood years before just how much they needed to hear words of appreciation from their father.

But it really isn't enough for us to applaud our loved ones simply for what they do. We need to move our appreciation up to another level, applauding them for who they are—a special person created in the image of God. This means expressions of pride, of gratitude, and of affection that are not linked to actions or accomplishments. It simply means, "I love you because you are you, and there's no one else like you in the world."

This is a particularly important responsibility for fathers, and it is irretrievably linked to the issue of prevention of homosexuality. Virtually every publication regarding the roots of homosexuality, whether published by gays or by others, points to the father-son relationship as being a primary factor in the development of same-sex attraction.

In *How Fathers Raise Homosexual Sons*, Dr. Toby Bieber writes, "It's true that mothers may be very destructive, but the point is that the fathers can defend the children. The importance of sound fathering has been recognized for a long time. As Sigmund Freud put it, 'I could not point to any need in childhood as strong as that for a father's protection.' Over and over, psychiatrists told us in much the same words: 'I never saw a homosexual who had a good relationship with his father.'"

In fact, recent research has shown that fathers actually seem to have absolute veto power over the homosexual development of their sons. And this is not accomplished through criticism, demands, humiliation, or other control measures. Bieber's team wrote in its study:

> We have come to the conclusion that a constructive, supportive, warmly related father precludes the possibility of a homosexual son; he acts as a neutralizing, protective agent should the mother make seductive or close-binding attempts.
>
> It is the loving quality of the fathering which a boy receives, and sometimes even the mere memory of it as reinforced by the mother, that now turns out to be a vital factor. Sons must be able to admire and identify with their fathers in order to become well-adjusted heterosexual males.[4]

Fathers play an incomparable role in the lives of young men and women, and affirmation of their children is one of their essential responsibilities. It is interesting to note that the voice of God the Father speaks audibly three times in the New Testament. On every occasion, he is speaking about his Son, and the voice was heard by those in the immediate vicinity. Now, to my way of thinking, when the voice of God is heard audibly, we should snap to attention, hear what he has to say, and, in this case, find out what we can learn from his example.

After Jesus was baptized by John in the Jordan River, God the Father said, "Thou art My beloved Son, in Thee I am well-pleased" (Mark 1:11, NASB).

On the Mount of Transfiguration, God the Father said, "This is My beloved Son, listen to Him!" (Mark 9:7, NASB).

Before the crucifixion, when Jesus prayed, "Father, glorify Thy name," God the Father answered, "I have both glorified it [through You], and will glorify it again" (John 12:28, NASB). God let the whole world know that Jesus' life had fulfilled his expectation and caused his name to be glorified.

> *The perfect and ideal Father, God, affirmed his Son, and he did it publicly.*

If Jesus' Father deemed it important to audibly affirm his Son, even when that Son was in his thirties, what can we say for ourselves? We earthly fathers should affirm our sons and daughters all their lives.

Dad As Head of the House

The biblical passage that best describes the function of a spiritual family is found in Ephesians 5:21–33. This scripture places a solemn admonition on the husband to love his wife as Jesus loved the Church and gave himself for her. Clearly, that responsibility entails a lot of giving of one's self to measure up to such a supreme example. A husband must really have the best interest of each member of the family at heart, and he must be willing to place himself in a serving role.

God has placed men at the head of the family, and with that role comes privilege and responsibility. It is a privilege to serve as a godly example of righteousness and to be an earthly reflection of Jesus caring for his Church, a model which the rest of the family can look up to and pattern their actions after.

Being the head of the house is not a matter of proving that we are more powerful than the rest of the members of our family and demanding their respect. Instead it means setting a loving example and creating a climate in which the family can function with love and respect for each other. Each husband and father has the honor of being a "servant-leader" of his household.

The wife also has a very important position in being "subject to [her] own husband, as to the Lord." Further on in this passage we read, "Let the wife see to it that she respect her husband." This role will not be difficult for her if the husband is the pacesetter, genuinely loving his wife and family in actions as well as in words. Ephesians 5:21 states, "Be subject to one another in the fear [respect] of Christ" (NASB). This applies to every family member, especially to husbands and wives. Finally, the following chapter begins with the words, "Children, obey your parents in the Lord, for this is right."

We can view all these admonitions as very difficult and forbidding, or we can view them as God's formula for a healthy, functional family. But one hypothetical question comes to mind when I reflect on all this: if families were to function by God's formula, I wonder if we would be having the problems in our society that we are now seeing?

Taking One Another Seriously

As I poured Sam a fresh cup of coffee, I thought back on the state of his family and how much change I was asking him to digest. As I sat down I said, "Well, Sam, are you up to exploring our need of being taken seriously?"

He sipped from the steaming mug and smiled, "I want to hear what you've got to say about that, Don. What exactly do you mean? When I hear the word seriously I think of somebody who is grim, hard, unpleasant, stern, critical, and even sour. As a matter of fact, I've been told that that's the way I have been viewed by certain members of my family at times. So is that the next thing you wanted me to confess to?"

"No, Sam, not at all. When I say that we all need to be taken seriously, I mean that we need to feel important, to feel respected, to feel our contributions are of value, and perhaps most importantly, not to feel we are mocked or ridiculed."

"Oh, yes," Sam sighed. "You're right. That's a really important need." And in his eyes, I could see that he knew all too well what he was talking about.

Being taken seriously is, in fact, serious business. People who aren't taken seriously can feel assaulted, as if they've been mugged and left for dead, their life draining out through spiritual wounds. If a person has been mocked, belittled, ignored, or otherwise overlooked, what usually is left for counselors to deal with is either a bitter, angry, and rebellious person or a depressed person.

No matter what the issue, no matter how it is expressed, both husbands and wives need to know that their opinions matter, and that their ideas, thoughts, and views are not falling on deaf ears. Of course, at times the comments of spouses, particularly those that have to do with personal issues, may sound more like nagging or criticism than simply a matter of opinion. Nonetheless, those opinions deserve a hearing, a discussion, and—if necessary—a change of heart.

Honestly speaking for myself and other men I have known, we males tend to have a big problem in this area, and I'm sorry to report that at times I've been at the front of the line. One would think, after years of seeking my wife's input and finding out how valuable it is, after witnessing time and again how right and right-on she is a very high percentage of the time, that I would applaud her suggestions. But I don't, at least not always. I'm not sure if it's a cultural thing, manly pride, or just my old sin nature sticking its head up.

Wives find this particular weakness in their husbands to be incredibly frustrating. As with listening and appreciating, taking another person seriously (or not doing so) usually stems from a pattern that was ingrained in us during our childhood. That is why we rarely see it in ourselves—it seems so "normal."

Of course, the more headway I make in this area, the more Diana and I are able to function as a team. She has my ear because she has my best interest—our best interest—at heart, and she has come to believe that I take her seriously. When we come to an impasse on a certain decision, she allows me to make the final choice. Because of past experience, my wife has confidence that I will hear her side and sincerely take it into consideration. Fortunately, such impasses take place infrequently. After so many years of marriage, we have established a working relationship where we almost always come to the same conclusion.

And it isn't just wives and husbands who need to be taken

seriously, either. All too often it is children and adolescents who are the most injured by our careless or even cruel behavior. Sometimes mocking is done in the name of family humor, and it is one of the very worst things a parent or caretaker can do. This is particularly the case if the mocking or teasing takes the form of labeling a developing child, even though it may seem funny to adults at the time. Blameworthy parents often brush it aside with some statement like, "No harm done—she knows we're teasing her," or "Don't worry about him—he knows we love him."

This is particularly problematic when, as far as emotional damage is concerned, the same-sex parent is the guilty party. In her book, *Homosexuality: A New Christian Ethic*, Elizabeth Moberly says, "From amidst a welter of details, one constant underlying principle suggests itself; that the homosexual—whether man or woman—has suffered from some deficit in the relationship with the parent of the same sex; and that there is a corresponding drive to make good this deficit—through the medium of same-sex, or 'homosexual,' relationships. . . . The primary cause of homosexuality is not an absent same-sex parent, but the child's defensive detachment toward him or her."[5]

Great harm is done with careless words. And the labels we place on others leave deep, unhealed scars. Cruel labeling has an especially devastating effect on developing children. Someone once said, "Sticks and stone will break your bones, but words will break your heart." Here is just a sampling of what we've heard in forty years of ministering to people:

You're so stupid.
What a dummy!

You fatty.
You big sissy.
What a klutz!
You lazy good-for-nothing.
What are you, retarded?
You little tramp!
Faggot!

Labels like these, placed on adolescents who lack a healthy sense of their own identity, mold them, convince them, deceive them, draw them into lifetime roles and lifestyle decisions that should never have occurred to them. Whatever the intention of the caregiver, such verbal abuse can really "set the stage" for some deadly addictive behaviors—such as homosexuality—which may never be broken or healed.

I have talked with hundreds of gay men over the years, and not one has escaped being ostracized, or being called a "sissy" or a "faggot," or having some other kind of deeply wounding experience. —Ram Dass in Gay Soul[6]

By contrast, the development of healthy behavior and self-esteem in children and youth comes from a balance between correction (discipline) and positive reinforcement from loving parents or other caretakers. And the same rules apply to single parents, blended families, or "normal" families where both parents are present.

"Praise whatever they are doing right" is a valuable motto, which clearly indicates an attempt to take another person seriously, too often nonexistent both in the home and in the workplace. We find it remarkably easy to tell those close to us that something is being done wrong. How often do we affirm them when they do something well? Are we praising one child more than another?

Both our spouses and our children feel that we take them seriously when we invite them to participate in family decisions. Once while our sons were still in high school, we asked them how they thought we should vote on the candidates and the issues in an upcoming election. Well, they suggested a couple of items that ol' Dad had not intended to vote for. Because of their interest and informed responses, I ended up voting according to their suggestions. This simple decision gave them confidence, respect, and a feeling that they had made a significant contribution.

Above all else, spouses and our children need to feel we are their personal cheerleaders. They need to realize that we will display unconditional love for them in both words and actions regardless of their present state of development. They need to know that they can count on us—regardless. They need for us to affirm their God-given dignity and the value he places on each individual he creates.

The three simple principles I spelled out for Sam are easy to talk about. And for some fortunate people, they are easily done. They are biblical in the sense that they demonstrate love toward others, they force us to think of others "more highly" than we think of ourselves, they demand that we treat others as we would want to be treated, and they require us to act according to God's principles.

And what if we don't decide to put them into practice?

The spouse who has not experienced this kind of love and grace rages or withdraws, feels hatred or indifference, fires off volleys of angry words or erects a solid wall of self-protection. The child or youth may react even more dramatically.

Hard experience has taught me that the stage gets set for all sorts of dangerous and self-destructive behaviors through family interaction or lack thereof. It begins early, and it continues to erode a life for decades, perhaps forever. As the destructive behavior plays out, it leaves some deep ruts in the brain and deep-rooted damage to the emotions—habits and hurts that are very hard, from a human perspective, to reverse. I have seen a handful of miracle people who have made a turnaround and are now very productive and healthy. These are women and men who have experienced forgiveness and reconciliation through a personal commitment to Jesus Christ as Lord of their lives.

But many others head down the road to addictions, promiscuity, homosexuality, and even suicide. Too often, they have not been listened to. They have not been appreciated. They have not been taken seriously.

My friend Sam and his family had begun to form some dangerous patterns which were still in a stage where they could be reversed without a miracle, if Sam would assume a loving leadership role in changing them.

Chapter Seven

Making a Change, Making a Difference

"Hi, Sam! How did your week go?"

Sam ran his fingers through his hair. "Much better than I expected, Don. Like you suggested, I tried making an effort to really listen to my wife. I actually tried sitting down after supper, asking her how her day went, and letting her know I was listening to her responses. I have to confess, it was the first time we've talked in years without my trying to read the newspaper and stave off her questions at the same time. And you were right—she has seemed a lot more pleasant. In fact, a couple of times she's given me a smile I haven't seen for a very long time."

"So you're doing okay with the 'servant-leader' role in your family?"

Sam nodded, chuckling a little at my choice of words, "I guess that's what men are supposed to be, isn't it?"

"It really is, Sam. And as you continue to make positive

changes in relating and in building up your family members, I believe they will respond in the same way to you. Just be sure you're sincere in your efforts. Families—especially kids—can smell a phony, self-centered person a mile away. And if they do, they'll really get turned off. By the way, how's the relationship with your son? You indicated last week that you thought he might have homosexual tendencies."

"Oh, he hasn't really said he is in so many words, but he and I sure don't mix at all. I know you don't like labeling, Don, but to be honest, he's what I call a sissy. I've tried shaming him; I've tried threatening him; I've tried challenging him to play me one-on-one in some sport of his choice. I even asked him to go with me over to the wrestling matches at the fairgrounds. I tried to tell him how exciting wrestling is to watch, but all I ever get is, 'Sorry, Dad, but I'm not really interested.'"

"Can't you find something else to do together?"

Sam shook his head sadly. "Well, he tried to get me to take him to the theater to see some stuffy play or actor or some boring dramatic performance. Why can't he be interested in normal male things like I am? Why can't he be a real man?"

Sam fixed his eyes on me, and he asked, a little sarcastically, "Sounds like your boys are pretty normal. Any ideas to help me, Don?"

Checking Out Our Motives

As I told Sam, before we even begin to look at specific preventative measures, we have to be very careful about our motives. In Matthew 6:1–5, Jesus gives the indication that our motives are more important to him than our actions:

"Be careful not to do your 'acts of righteousness' before men, to be seen by them. If you do, you will have no reward from your Father in heaven.

"So when you give to the needy, do not announce it with trumpets, as the hypocrites do in the synagogues and on the streets, to be honored by men. I tell you the truth, they have received their reward in full. But when you give to the needy, do not let your left hand know what your right hand is doing, so that your giving may be in secret. Then your Father, who sees what is done in secret, will reward you.

"And when you pray, do not be like the hypocrites, for they love to pray standing in the synagogues and on the street corners to be seen by men. I tell you the truth, they have received their reward in full."

In discussing the two "biggies" of what we Christians seem to think of as important religious acts—giving money and praying to God—Jesus makes it quite clear that if our motive is simply to look good in the eyes of others, there will be no further reward from the Father. In the same way, taking steps to "fix" our children isn't a sideshow that we put on for our friends or church acquaintances, intended to make them think better of us. Nor is it a means of ending our embarrassment with our kids if they don't quite measure up to our ideas about "real men" or "ladylike young women."

Unselfishness is a key element in true Christianity. In Philippians 2, Paul cites the example set by Jesus, illustrating what it means to live an unselfish life. "Each of you should look not only to your own interests, but also to the interests of others" (v. 4). Paul goes on to say that we should regard one another as more important than ourselves.

These are essential principles in all human relationships. They are particularly important in marriage and parenting, and they are incredibly significant when we are dealing with those special people we have a particularly hard time loving. We sometimes have difficulty nurturing our children if they remind us of others or ourselves. We should not be surprised when the very qualities we've hated in ourselves and others reemerge in the children we've parented, but we must guard against reacting to this by pushing them away.

In a relationship like Sam's, a very common dynamic is unmistakable—the less nurturing Sam is to his son, the more his son may eventually be attracted to the homosexual lifestyle. In his book *Parents on Trial*, David Wilkerson makes a rather startling statement: "The real tragedy of homosexuality is that with a little understanding, love, and help from the parents of these victims, this would not have happened at all."[1]

In their book *Growing Up Straight*, Peter and Barbara Wyden echo Wilkerson's premise: "No parent sets out deliberately to produce a delinquent—or a homosexual. Yet it is recognized today that delinquency and homosexuality are both rooted in the home. This brings us to a phenomenon that is still considered somewhat mysterious by some people. Why does one son become a professor, while his brother turns into a gangster? And how can the same parents raise a homosexual and also a heterosexual son?"[2]

The answer lies, of course, in the fact that a father may treat each son and daughter differently. Or, even though he treats them all the same way, one child may react differently from another. For example, a father I once knew had three sons—two were aggressive, hard-nosed characters and the third was artistic and sensitive. The father never communicated acceptance to any of the three boys, but the sensitive one seemed to be affected the most by the father's rejection. Even in his mid-fifties, he is still making an extreme effort to get verbal approval from his dad. He has, to this day, never received it. The other two sons haven't received the old man's approval either, but it doesn't seem to matter to them one way or the other.

Unbeknownst to them, parents do, in fact, react to each of their children in a different way. This is not damaging *per se*. But the chances are that children who become homosexuals have been singled out by an unhealthy parent in an unhealthy way. "A child's homosexual tendencies are a symptom of parental disturbance," said Dr. Toby Bieber.

When parents are confused about why one of their children had serious problems and the other did not, they may blame outside forces. I often hear that people with problems (criminal or sexual) are unfortunates who "fell in with bad company," as if they had no built-in selection system which determined their choices. The research I have looked at has shown otherwise: the parent unknowingly creates vulnerability to seduction (criminal or sexual).

In a large number of instances, no male role model existed during early childhood developmental years in the home, whether it be father, father substitute or older male sibling. This absence of male role models with whom to identify was even more characteristic of the most severely disturbed effeminate boys. In cases where the father or a father surrogate was present in the home, he was typically described as psychologically remote from the family.
—George Rekers[3]

Hard Parent, Tender Child

Investigating the subject of preventing homosexuality, we have researched thousands of books and publications written by authors who are homosexual or who write about this issue. We have interviewed numerous men and women struggling with homosexuality, and we have also spoken with their counselors. A common denominator that consistently emerges is one of personality type: the controlling, domineering father or mother and that parent's impact on the sensitive child. During the process one of our researchers remarked, "I'm sure there are exceptions, but at this point I haven't run into any."

Over the years, I have developed a study of personality types, and it has been helpful to me in my counseling work. Let's start with a list of characteristics depicting the Controlling/Domineering personality type, which I have observed to be the most explosive:

- Cool—tough—detached—hard

- Often runs over others—exercises power and control over people/situations

- Independent—difficult to get close to

- Businesslike—impersonal—appears to treat people as things

- Impatient—disciplined in the use of time

- Risk taker—competitive in relationships

- Enjoys having power—likes to make decisions independently of others

Now let's contrast this personality type with the complete opposite. Here are some characteristics of the Amiable/ Sensitive type of person, who is often also artistic.

- Easygoing—friendly
- Warm personality—cooperative
- Interested in people as people—likes to belong to groups
- Close relationships and friendships are important
- Undisciplined about time—appears slow in actions
- Is not a risk taker—not concerned about controlling others
- Needs emotional support and validation

The question is, of course, how does the sensitive child react to the domineering parent? How does he or she feel? What thoughts go through his or her head? Here are some reactions this child will most likely experience:

- You make me feel guilty, and you misunderstand me.
- You don't trust me—you're disappointed in me.
- You are overbearing and ruthless.
- You are overly demanding and never satisfied.
- You make me feel inadequate.

If the developing child possesses a majority of the "Amiable/Sensitive" characteristics, one can see very quickly why that child will feel alienated and will perceive rejection from the controlling, strong-willed parent.

It is important to note that problems arise from how the child perceives adult actions and words, more than what the adult actually does or means to do. *Perception trumps everything.* Perception is what really counts to our children—it is what they hear and feel. If they feel genuine unconditional love for who they really are inside, that sense of acceptance then allows them to respond and to develop in a healthy way. Unfortunately, that is not always the case.

A professor of education at a university related in one of his classes: "I have seen many creative four-year-olds, but very few creative twenty-four-year-olds." Why is this true?

A high school teacher relates that a large percentage of freshman are entering high school with a very negatively warped view of life, including disrespect for other people and for property. These students, mainly fourteen-year-olds, display a prevailing state of anger, which can be set off for no apparent reason or logic. Why is this happening?

One reason repeats itself again and again, in families that vary from poor to rich, from poorly educated to highly academic and literate. All too often, a creative, developing child gets "squashed" by controlling parents. This youngster is continually suppressed into a meaningless and purposeless existence. By the time youngsters like this hit ninth grade, they have been beaten down so long that they just don't have the motivation to get up anymore. In other cases, they rebel and get sucked into addictive behaviors, which in turn bring on more overwhelming control from the adult caretakers in their life.

Fathers and Sons

. . . [In] a study of 40 homosexual males . . . there was not a single case in which the homosexual reported having had

Let's be more specific. Rather than speaking in generalities, let's take a look at the impact of a domineering father on a sensitive male child.

- In the developing son's eyes, the domineering father becomes bigger than life. Dad is someone from whom the boy will never be able to get needed healthy attention. He doesn't even imagine that he will ever even feel liked by his father. The son's greatest longing is to receive acceptance and appreciation from his adult hero, but in this scenario the child does not receive it. In this situation, the stage is set for the child to seek others who will meet those needs. And, as is often the case, an older male homosexual is available to do what the father failed to do—convey love and acceptance.

- Because the father is highly critical, the child will feel everything he attempts is unsatisfactory. For example, after one son did his weekly chore of cutting the lawn, the father flew into a rage over a tuft of grass that was missed. Another young man explains, "My father ridiculed me constantly. He even ridiculed the very few things I was good at."

- A sensitive son's self-esteem may be crushed because, when he chooses to avoid physical confrontations and turns his back on playground fights, his father calls him a sissy and a coward.

- A son's relationship with his father may be destroyed in the confusion that results when the father projects his anger toward his own hated father or brother onto his sensitive son.

- The son may feel alienated instead of accepted by a father who appears to be indifferent, uninvolved, and rejecting, sometimes deriding the son for his lack of interest in "typical" masculine activities.

- If a father in an unhappy marriage feels rejected by his wife, and she focuses all her attention on the sensitive son, the result may be that the father/son relationship becomes competitive. This father may unconsciously look upon this son as a sexual rival and express hostility, rejection, or indifference toward him. The feelings of competition and fear of attack from the father are in opposition to the son's wish for his love and acceptance. These conflicting emotions hamper the son's developing masculine sexuality, and this lack of identification with masculinity can also be offensive to the father.

Fathers and Daughters

Just as a domineering father may have a profound effect on a sensitive son, he will also impact a daughter with a gentle and unassertive personality. (Identifying a woman as belonging to the "gentle and unassertive" personality type can be difficult because they sometimes surround themselves with aggressive-looking defense mechanisms as time goes on, and they may not always appear gentle and unassertive by nature.)

- In the eyes of a sensitive girl, a domineering father may be viewed as puritanical, overly possessive, and inhibiting of her development as a woman.

- The sensitive girl will probably be afraid of her controlling father, even though he may not be threatening her physically.

- Her perception will be that he usually disapproves of and belittles her friends.

- The daughter often pictures her father as hostile, detached, gruff, and crude.

- The father-daughter relationship is likely to be distant and lacking in affection.

- If the father is alcoholic and physically abusive, this further distorts the daughter's opinion of men and of herself in relation to them.

- Ultimately, a domineering father damages his sensitive daughter, usually driving her away from men in an effort to avoid further pain. This sometimes leads to same-sex attractions. The opposite consequence may also result if she turns toward promiscuous heterosexuality, pursuing a lifelong search for the male affection and acceptance she did not receive from her father.

Angela Ludwig in the book *Striving for Gender Identity* states, "Closeness with heterosexual men and the experience of acceptance and understanding is fundamentally important for the healing/developing process. . . . Homosexuality is a symbolic act that represents an attempt to find one's own wholeness."[5]

By the time we had finished discussing some of the behaviors and traits of children with controlling fathers, Sam was feeling very uncomfortable. "I think my kids must be doomed," he said, looking resigned and depressed.

"Don't be too hard on yourself, Sam," I smiled. "Maybe I've beat you up a little as a dad, but don't forget there are at least two parents involved with every child, and mothers play an important role too."

"When it comes to the kids," Sam volunteered, "my wife is a saint. She's the most loving and gentle person on earth . . ."

"That's good, Sam, and you and your kids should be thankful, because a domineering mother can have a very detrimental impact on her children as well."

Sam raised his eyebrows, glad to see the buck passed beyond his particular realm of responsibility. "So tell me. What happens with domineering mothers?"

"Well, for one thing, it's worse," I explained, "when the father is passive."

"I may be a lot of things," Sam grinned in relief, "but passive isn't one of them."

Mothers and Sons

Just as a controlling father has a profound effect on his son, a domineering mother and a passive father make an equally troublesome impact on the male child. Here are some of the results of such an arrangement:

- Neither the mother nor the father encourages masculine attitudes or activities in their son.

- Most of the time, all decision making is left to the mother, so the son has no decisive male role model to follow.

- He may come to view himself as fragile if the mother seems unduly concerned about protecting him from physical injury. One troubled young man told us, "My mother always treated me as an invalid and hoped I'd never be well enough to leave her."

- A domineering mother can make the developing male child feel overprotected, excessively dependent, favored and babied, openly preferred to the husband.

- He may become confused and conflicted about his role if his mother behaves in a seductive way, caressing him a lot and asking him to give her massages. At times a mother may inappropriately turn her attentions toward her son when she cannot get love from her husband.

- The son may feel rejected, minimized, detached, or fearful if the mother projects hostility on him because she was unloved or rejected by her own mother or because she harbors resentment against, or outright hatred for, her own father.

The "classical" homosexual triangular pattern is one where the mother is . . . dominant and minimizing toward a husband who is a detached father, particularly a hostile detached one. —Irving Bieber[6]

Dr. Bieber suggests that many of these mothers single out a son who reminds them of their own fathers or brothers. Because of their emotional problems, these mothers have an unconscious wish to "possess" these beloved males, and they transfer this wish upon the singled-out son.

The most damaging result of such parental behavior, of course, is that the son's masculinity is badly distorted. These young men may experience gender confusion, inability to assert themselves, misogyny, effeminacy, and same-sex emotional attractions. In short, an overly dominate mother can propel her son toward the homosexual lifestyle.

One fifty-year-old ex-homosexual man related to me how his mother's vicious verbal attacks about his inability to write clearly still haunt him today, although she has been dead for ten years. She constantly demeaned him, pointing out that his efforts did not meet her expected standards and that they never would. Likewise, she also attacked the father, demoralizing and controlling him through criticism as well.

Mothers and Daughters

How do these same mothers affect their daughters, particularly when the father is passive?

- Because her excessively bossy, hypercritical, domineering mother demands the center of the family's attention, The daughter learns to focus her attention away from her own needs.

- The daughter is often maneuvered away from developing a healthy relationship with the father when such a mother derogates her husband by verbal tactics. She may openly ridicule and mock her spouse with insults such as "You loser, you're worthless," or "Do you call yourself a man?" She may even abuse him physically in front of their daughter to establish her power.

- A father who accepts a passive role and allows an aggressive spouse to cause destructive turmoil in their home may disappoint his daughter so profoundly that she may become infuriated, even to the point of attacking him physically. "Be a man!" the daughter wants to scream. "Take my side! Defend me!"

- However, a daughter may also defend her father, taking his side in an argument against her mother. She does so in the hope that this will stiffen his spine and strengthen his resolve to stand up to the mother. Instead, he usually backs down and leaves the daughter exposed to the domineering mother's vindictiveness.

Clearly, this situation sets the stage for such a daughter to have grave difficulties relating to any man in a healthy way.

"So, Sam, that's a quick overview of some very dangerous family dynamics, and I can see that some of them hit close to home. Now here's the big question: What specific adjustments in your attitude and actions are you willing to make?"

Sam looked at me rather blankly. "I can't even imagine where I should start."

"Well, when I was in the Navigators, Bob Foster had a saying. He always reminded us that 'The basics are still basic.' Even though your situation is unique, there are some positive and transformative things you can do that all parents should keep in mind, no matter what the situation."

"What kind of things are you talking about, Don? Are these basics for keeping kids out of homosexuality?"

"I guess you might say that they are the elements for being a good dad to any kid, boy or girl, young or old."

And with that, I offered Sam my list of Ten Preventative Parenting Principles. "We've been talking about homosexuality," I explained, "but these principles can prevent much more than that—misunderstandings, quarrels, bitterness, and any number of other family troubles."

Sam looked genuinely interested and reached for his pen.
"Shall I write them down?"

"You don't need to, Sam. This is your very own copy, ready to
stick on the refrigerator door."

Ten Preventative Parenting Principles

1. Treat your children the way you like to be treated. Jesus
   gave us the Golden Rule as a gauge for all kinds of inter-
   personal relationships, including parenting. Do you like
   to receive compliments? Your child does too. Do you like
   to have someone show genuine interest in your hobby,
   likes and dislikes, social interests? Show genuine interest in your child's activities.
2. Allow children to make mistakes and still retain their
   dignity. Mistakes can be great learning opportunities for
   facing challenges together.
3. Give them breathing room to develop in a natural way.
   Children need time and space to formulate their own
   convictions.
4. Shore up their weaknesses by appreciating their
   strengths. Every strength has an offsetting weakness,
   and vice versa. Do not major on the weakness, but major
   on their special, individual strengths.
5. Display unconditional love and acceptance. Be sure the
   love you communicate to a son or daughter is directed
   toward their specific person and personality—who they
   are, not just what they do.
6. Be with them—take them with you. Become involved in
   their interests, and do things together. If you'll hang out
   together, you'll learn to enjoy what they enjoy.
7. Don't be afraid to expose your vulnerable side. It's okay

for a man to have fears and tears and share them with a son or a daughter. It's okay for a mother to lose her temper or cry in frustration. Don't dump on the kids, but be transparent, so you can identify with their emotions when the time comes.

8. Be open and honest about personal struggles. This requires discernment and wisdom, but sharing personal concerns—to a point—draws you closer to your children and encourages them to confide in you.

9. Affirm that your relationship with them is more important than any issue. Regardless of disagreements, disappointments, or even dismay over their choices and ideas, always let your children know that you will love them forever—no matter what they do.

10. Make sure your children know that they are a very high priority in your life.

Finding Proper Priorities

Principle number ten brings us to another key issue, one that goes beyond family life and spills over into business, church, community service, and friendships with others. This is a biblical approach I use to prioritize my life in a godly order, allowing everything to fall into its proper place. These priorities come from the conviction that all of life's functions are to be done as unto the Lord (Colossians 3:17). The priorities look like this:

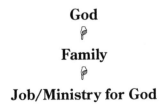

God

Family

Job/Ministry for God

When push comes to shove with children, what gets bumped? My real priorities are not necessarily reflected in what I may say or think I believe. They are more accurately seen in what I actually do and in what gets my attention.

When the boys were young, Diana and I hosted a Bible study in our home with several other couples. We told the boys that if they needed our attention, they should come into the room and stand quietly. If I saw them standing there, it was my cue to take a ten-minute break and get involved in their homework, provide some kind of permission, offer advice, or do whatever else they needed from their dad.

Although it wasn't the primary purpose, this particular arrangement proved to be an excellent example of proper priorities for the young couples who were attending the Bible study. Through our family situation, the couples were able to see that our sons' needs were a higher priority than theirs, even a higher priority than our ministry.

Can People Change?

I shared with Sam—and with you—some personality profiles that often appear in families with problems. I've learned all too well that neglecting certain traits in our personalities can fill my life and our family's life with pain. This is true, irrespective of anyone's financial, ethnic, or cultural background.

When I present the personality profiles to various groups or counselees, the common response I hear from domineering adults is "But you don't understand. That's my temperament or personality type—I can't help it! *I can't change it!*"

You know what? I used to say the same thing and give the same excuse. As a matter of fact, as far as the domineering father is concerned, I would have to say that I was among the worst for a good part of my boys' lives.

My own life as a boy comprised a lot of hard, physical work. Along with the overwhelming work ethic they enforced, my parents made it clear that I was not allowed to express feelings of any kind, even when afflicted with severe pain. I was told—repeatedly—that "real men don't cry, whimper, or complain." And real men get their work done regardless, no excuses. The hero of the day in our Central California farming culture was John Wayne. He was rough and tough, with no emotions standing in his way.

Although I was a high achiever in school and received many awards, the adults in my life did not give out praise for "performance." The only two "compliments" I finally received from them when I was much older turned out to be rather questionable as well. Diana heard one of them: "It's about time you finished that job" (high praise from my point of view), and she quickly informed me, "Don, that was not a compliment!" My reply was, "It's close enough dear—let me treasure it as such."

I'm not sure just how much of my family history influenced my personality/temperament or if I was just born that way. But on a scale of one to ten, I'd call myself a "10+ Driver/Type A." If somebody happened to comment, "That task is impossible," I would immediately reply, "But *I* haven't tried it yet." I allowed no such thing in my thinking process as "it cannot be done." Sad to say, that also reflected on how I related to people and how I drove my family and ministry.

No human alive could measure up to my standards and expectations—including myself! I was a world-class expert on how to criticize and put people down, regardless of their good performance. I was even less able to see any good in another person's inner character or to show appreciation, complimenting them for being who they were—a woman, man, or child made in the image of God.

Around the time our sons started high school, God started getting my attention. He somehow managed to make it clear to me that if I did not deal with my outbursts of anger, I was going to lose my sons. He made me understand that their spirits would not survive any more trampling by their father's insensitive stampedes.

One day I was grappling with this idea while working with our livestock. I became so infuriated with a frisky (and, in my opinion, not very bright) ram sheep that I threw a stone at it. Since I was a poor shot, I missed it and hit a innocent little lamb in the head instead, knocking it out cold. I thought I had killed the lamb. In the midst of that bizarre situation, I came to the final conclusion that my anger really was out of control. It occurred to me that Jesus is portrayed in Scripture as a lamb, and that lambs are harmless, loving animals. Without question, I needed to deal with my rage immediately, if not sooner.

Up until that time I had always justified my actions with the usual cop-out, "It's just the way I am." But fortunately, I had committed myself to the process of growing in my faith by examining the Scriptures and seeking to "walk as Jesus walked" in my personal life.

In the Gospels, I learned that James and John were called "the sons of thunder" by Jesus in the early part of his ministry (Mark 3:17). Apparently they, too, had explosive temperaments. Later on, however, John was described as the "Disciple of Love." A drastic change had occurred in John's life because of his close and constant relationship with Jesus.

In Oswald Chambers's book *Daily Thoughts for Disciples,* he observes:

> Remember, the battle is in the will; whenever we say "I can't," or whenever we are indifferent, it means "I won't." It is better to let Jesus Christ uncover the obstinacy. If there is one point where we say "I won't" then we shall never know His Power. From the moment that God uncovers a point of obstinacy in us and we refuse to let Him deal with it, we begin to be skeptical, to sneer and watch for defects in the lives of others. But when we yield to Him entirely, He makes us blameless in our personal lives, in our practical lives, and in our profound lives. It is not done by piety; it is wrought in us by the sovereign grace of God, and we have not the slightest desire to trust in ourselves in any degree, but in Him alone.[7]

I also came face-to-face with the New Testament teaching that the same power that raised Jesus up from the dead is available to us. Through this power, God has made it possible for us to live a life that pleases him (Romans 6:4–11; Philippians 3:10–16). The real issue for me was whether I would choose to accept and appropriate that available resurrection power and to make the daily effort of reflecting the character of Jesus as revealed in the Gospels.

Would I give God permission to totally invade my life?

For me, the answer was yes.

My reasoning and excuses for being "just the way I am" were shattered, and I discovered that I needed a complete overhaul. When I chose to let God begin the change process, I found myself becoming a loving father to my family and a caring and encouraging person to those around me. I gradually learned that I could be a man and still be tender. I knew that, if the situation demanded it, I could (and should) operate on a tough-love basis.

At first, of course, this was very uncomfortable. I could no longer control those around me through my usual hardline tactics and angry outbursts, practices that I had developed in childhood. Diana relates that the change in my life really threw her a curve because it came about so suddenly. But she did like the new man I was becoming. I began to like myself better too and wondered why I had been so self-centered, power hungry, and controlling. Why hadn't I given my family the husband and father that God intended for them to have all along?

The showing of affection towards others was the next item on God's program of my development. He insisted that I become more like the living Christ in my dealings with people. Diana and I had a discipleship ministry at a university during the 1960s Jesus Movement. One of the trademarks of the movement was the expression of outward affection by both men and women. Well, ol' stiff Don here realized, first of all, that he had a handicap in this area, and it really showed.

I did come to my senses about that matter and arrived at the conclusion that if Jesus and his disciples could show affection, it was perfectly all right for me to do likewise. It took a while to loosen up, but before long I learned to respond with a warm hug. Today, more than three decades later, I can verify that it wasn't a passing phase I was going through. God did, indeed, change me from the inside out. Now when I meet, listen to, and admonish dominating, controlling men and women, I really do understand how they feel. I also know, beyond the shadow of a doubt, what God wants to accomplish in their hearts, their lives, and their families.

When Sam was about ready to leave, he leaned over and said, "You know what really scares me, Don?"

"Tell me," I prodded him.

"I'm really afraid I'll lose control of everything and everybody in my family if I change, or become more loving, or whatever it is you're trying to tell me to do. Were you able to keep control over your boys once you lightened up on them?"

I laughed out loud at Sam's predicament. "Let me tell you what happened," I began. "When both our sons reached their eighteenth birthdays, they decided to make an announcement *together. They explained that now they were adults, and they weren't going to operate under our family rules any longer. They specifically mentioned our rule about coming home at an agreed-upon hour and letting us know where they were going and what they were going to do.*

"Well, it just so happened on that same night that Diana and I went to a musical performance. We didn't tell them where we were going or that we might not return home until about two o'clock in the morning.

"At about midnight, they started to panic. And when we walked in at two we got a very harsh 'reaming' from our sons. My comment to them was simply: 'It doesn't feel good, does it? That's why we respect each other and keep everyone informed about where we are—that's what a family is all about.'

"Sam, we never had another problem with keeping control over their evening activities. They learned that common courtesy is an important part of family life. And I guess we learned how much they cared about us. Either way, from that time on, the controls came from love, not from anger or fear or tough talk."

Sam looked at me curiously. "So that works for you?"

"Sam, believe me. I wouldn't have it any other way."

Chapter Eight

More Than Meets the Eye

"Sam, you don't really think Jason is gay, do you?" Sam's minister, Pastor Bob, stared at Sam in utter disbelief. "If you don't mind my saying so, I find that impossible to believe."

Carl, Jason's youth pastor, simply raised his eyebrows slightly and said nothing. The four of us were meeting together at my suggestion, and with Sam's agreement, to discuss Jason's situation. Sam was more worried about Jason than ever because of an essay he'd found in the family computer. Jason had written about the pros and cons of same-sex relationships, and as far as Sam was concerned, it was the smoking gun he'd been looking for. His mind was made up. Jason was gay.

"Carl, have you had any reason to worry about Jason's sexuality?" I asked the youth pastor. I thought Carl would have noticed signs of gender confusion in Jason. He and I had worked together to formulate a list of warning signs for concerned adults.

Carl hesitated for a moment, and with an apologetic glance at Sam, he looked me in the eye. "Forgive me for saying so, but

I think the biggest problem Jason has is feeling like Sam here hates him. Jason is only fourteen years old, and I don't believe for a minute he's ever been attracted to anybody of the same sex. In fact, he's had a crush on Julie Parker for six months. Everybody in the youth group knows that."

Sam wasn't sure whether to be insulted or relieved. "What do you mean, he thinks I don't like him? Jason knows I love him."

Carl took a deep breath, looked at the pastor, looked at me, and finally fixed his eyes on Sam. "No, he doesn't. He thinks you hate him. He talks about it all the time. He knows you think he's 'faggy,' as you seem to have put it, and he thinks it's ridiculous."

There was a very uncomfortable silence.

"Sam," I interjected, "I know you've been putting into practice some of the things we've talked about. But you and Jason need to talk. It sounds like he needs some affirmation, and maybe even an apology."

Sam was enormously defensive by now, and he could hardly contain his anger. "I'm not apologizing to anybody! For one thing, I'd like to know why he's writing essays about homosexuality. For another, I'd like to know why you're laying all the blame for homosexuality on the parents' front doorstep. That's a lot of nonsense."

I nodded. "You're partly right, Sam. There are other factors. But families set the stage for each child's future. As it turns out, you don't have the kind of problem you thought you did. But you may be headed for some others—some of them just as deadly—if you don't work out your differences with your son."

There was another moment of cold silence, then Pastor Bob quietly asked, "Sam, aren't Jason and my daughter in the same current affairs class?"

"I guess so. Why?"

"Well, Melissa had an assignment last week to write about

the cultural pros and cons of homosexuality. I know, because we talked about it at dinner. Didn't Jason mention it to you?"

Sam, who had great respect for his pastor, looked a little sheepish. "We don't talk about things like that. Jason never tells me anything."

A few things went through my mind, and fortunately I didn't say any of them. Pastor Bob smiled and kindly suggested, "Maybe you should ask him, Sam. That would clear up one misunderstanding. But there's one thing I really want you to think about. There is no more important earthly relationship in your son's life than his relationship with you. He's a sensitive, talented boy, and his acting ability is really making an impression in the drama department at school. There's nothing wrong with acting, nothing unacceptable about it, and nothing 'gay' about it. I think it would make all the difference in the world if you would step up and support his interest in the theater. It's a gift God has given him, and it would be wrong if he didn't use it."

Sam was lost in thought for a long time. I could almost hear him swallowing his pride in large, uncomfortable lumps. Finally he stood up and looked at his watch. "Well, thanks guys. I guess I learned something today, and most of it was good. I'll think about what you said, Pastor," he said, extending his hand.

"You too, Don." He tossed me a half smile and headed for the door. Then he turned around. "Oh, Carl. What about this Julie? Do you know her family? What is she like?"

SAM AND I had spent considerable time talking about the role family plays in setting the stage for homosexuality. It's true the family is not the only factor involved in an individual's process of moving into homosexuality. Many authors, most notably Toby Bieber, Elizabeth Moberly, and George Rekers, make it very clear that no single issue alone—not even the major issue of family—creates a homo-sexual person.

One key influence is that of peer relationships and their impact on young, vulnerable adolescents. Author Gerard Van Den Aardweg explains:

> Peer relationships, in turn, can significantly influence the factor that is of paramount importance: the teenager's self view as to his masculinity or her femininity. In a girl, for example, apart from such factors as a lack of security in her relation with the mother, being the favorite of the father (or, on the contrary, being neglected by the father), quite differ-ent things can influence that self-view: teasing by peers, feel-ings of inferiority in relation to her siblings; physical clumsiness, "ugliness," that is, the perception of not being pretty or attractive in the eyes of boys during puberty; or hav-ing been viewed by family members as being boyish ("you are just like your uncle").
>
> One young man related this experience, "The other boys, who are more manly, are against me." His being called "sissy" reflects this, for the term does not mean being seen as a real girl, it means not being a normal man, being an inferior man. It is nearly synonymous with being a weakling, one who cries easily, as girls do, who does not fight but flees. [1]

A Constellation of Causes

Peer relationships. Societal influences. Molestation. The list of possible influences that set the stage for a homosexual condition goes on and on. I think that if we were to create an equation, we could give the family an 80 percent factor, and other outside influences combined, a 20 percent factor. But though we can't leave the family out of the equation, we can't ignore other causes either. I've mentioned some of the following factors in previous chapters, and I bring them up again because they need to be reconsidered from a different angle. Others I will introduce for the first time. Whether they have to do with the family or not, let's take a brief look at them, one by one.

The Individual Person's Self-will

God has made each of us unique and in possession of a free will. He allows us to choose to do whatever we want to do, whether it conforms to his ways or not. Young people sometimes make choices that simply do not reflect their parents' wishes or influence. Even if parents do all the right things, there are no guarantees our children will choose to live in a manner that meets with our approval, much less demands our applause.

The only guarantees we have are in God himself and his love for us. Even in the face of that love, we can choose to walk away from him. We are all free moral agents, not puppets of either a divine or a human order.

The real challenge for us as parents is to unconditionally love our offspring and communicate that love to them, even if their free-will choices do not reflect our values, standards, or goals in life.

Pornography

As I pointed out before, pornography is an unseen abscess in many lives. Both heterosexual and homosexual people get hooked into pornography's destructive and never-ending web. Porn has become a multi-billion dollar business available through magazines, movies, TV, the Internet, and the advertising industry. Even though it may be sampled in very small amounts to begin with, pornography is addictive, and in many cases it completely dominates and controls its victims. Far too many young people, particularly males, have gotten hooked into pornography after finding their fathers' hidden stash of magazines or videos. If Dad does it, it must be all right.

The pornography industry's publication Adult Video News (AVN) reports that industry revenues have doubled in five years, $2.1 billion to $4.2 billion . . . 697 million adult videos were rented during 1997.[2]

Media

Various representatives of today's media would have us believe that their message only reflects the standards society has already adopted. Experience would contradict them. The media—film, television, advertising, publishing, magazines, even fine art—seem to be forever pushing the moral envelope.[3] This provides our society—most notably our youth—with a very steady diet of desensitizing filth. A recent editorial points out that "movies shed so much light on American culture as it really is. Most of the time, their makers are simply trying to tell us what they think we want to hear."[4]

In suggested media tactics offered by the homosexual community to further their agenda, the following statement is made:
"In the average American household, the TV screen radiates its embracing bluish glow for more than fifty hours every week, bringing films, sitcoms, talk shows, and news

> *reports right into the living room. These hours are a*
> *gateway into the private world of straights, through which*
> *a Trojan horse might be passed. For once, Marshall*
> *McLuhan is right: where desensitization is concerned, the*
> *medium is the message . . . of normalcy."*
> —Marshall Kirk and Hunter Madsen [5]

Spousal Abuse in the Home

Although I have already looked at family dynamics as a source of trouble, I cannot stress enough the damage done by specific forms of domestic abuse. Our culture's epidemic of wife beating and other physical violence in the home contributes to the homosexual equation. Witnessing spousal abuse and desperately feeling responsible to stop it is not likely, on its own, to drive a young person toward same-sex relationships. But a boy or girl, who is already struggling with gender confusion and sees his father beating his mother (or vice versa) or sibling, may find one more reason to reject traditional heterosexual roles. Like most other factors, it becomes part of a constellation of causes, all of which feed on each other.

Verbal Abuse of the Father by the Mother

Again, some forms of domestic abuse take a particular toll in the area of gender confusion. One notable form is the "angry woman/broken man" pattern. Although males often carry out physical abuse in the home, verbal abuse is not infrequently the handiwork of females, and there is an aspect of this that has a direct link with homosexuality.

When a young boy sees his father berated, criticized, or mocked by his mother, he is—intentionally or unintentionally—thrust into the role of judging between the two. If the mother is dominant and the father is weak in the child's eyes, he will perceive that the father is being emotionally castrated by the mother. This may cause him to despise his father, because he is attracted to the mother's apparent strength. It may also confuse him about gender, the role of the male, and how he wants to see himself.

> Mothers who are continually involved in arguments with the father are likely to have sons who sympathize and identify with their hurt, particularly if the boy is close to them and has had little attachment to the father. What follows then is a mother and son united against the father. The boy will see masculinity as brutal and insensitive and be more inclined to reject his own manifestations of gender.
> —Joseph Nicolosi[6]

This, of course, is not to diminish the damage done by verbally abusive husbands or other males. Abuse is abuse and it is inexcusable, and angry words will cause deep damage. Because there is a unique dynamic between mothers and sons, a verbally abusive mother is particularly damaging to her son's gender identity when she has a dominant personality and directs her rage towards the boy's passive father.

Angry, abusive women are often following the example of their own mothers. Diana and I first encountered Sue on a university campus. This young woman had left a trail of chaos and broken relationships behind her because of her anger. When we tried to reach out to her, she quickly informed us that her parents had sent her to four different psychiatrists, all to no avail. Then she looked me straight in the eye and said, "Honey, what can you tell me about myself that those four shrinks couldn't?"

Without waiting for an answer, Sue began to berate her mother. Her angry diatribe went on for over thirty minutes, and during the course of our conversation, she called her mother every name I'd ever heard and a few original creations of her own.

Once she wound down I said, "Sue, let's say that you get married and have a daughter, and twenty years later she attends this university. I'm still here ministering to students, and she is sitting in the same chair you're sitting in right now. Do you have any idea what she might be saying about you, her mother? She would be saying the very same things in the same angry way that you're talking about your mother today. Don't you see what you're doing? If you keep heading in the same direction, you're going to be just like your mother."

Sue screamed, "Just like my mother?" She threw her hands in the air dramatically, and to my shock, she literally fell over backwards onto the floor. She got up, dusted herself off, and repeated, "Are you trying to tell me that I'm just like my mother?"

"You bet you are. That's exactly what I'm telling you. But you can change all that starting right now. You need to make a decision to deal with your anger, and you need to exercise forgiveness toward your mother. Then, and only then, can you make a 180-degree turnabout."

A week later, the University's Dean of Students phoned me, "Don, what's going on with Sue?"

My heart sank. I asked, "What do you mean? Now what's she done?"

"No, you don't understand," he said. "She came in yesterday and apologized for her bad behavior. She wanted to go on record that she has been a completely different person since her talk with you."

Ten years later, Sue herself called me. She thanked me for what I'd said to her that day and told me that she'd repented her rage and forgiven her mother. "I'm still really serious about my faith, and my anger toward my mother is completely gone. Don, I can never thank you enough."

Dealing with anger is one of the most important decisions any person can make. Every form of abuse—even sexual abuse—is rooted in hatred and rage, and the anger may be taken out on an innocent third party. If you are unable to resolve anger issues on your own, don't hesitate to seek counsel and help.

For the anger of man does not achieve the righteousness of God. (James 1:20, NASB)

Sexual Abuse and Pedophilia

If the real truth could only be known as to how much incest and sexual abuse really goes on, the world would be stunned. Those who work with youth are overwhelmed with the amount of molestation they hear about when young people begin to confide in them. Some counselors state that fifty percent or more of all females have been molested, most of them incestuously, before the age of twelve. However, no one really knows, because many victims are unwilling to talk about their experiences. Hidden or exposed, the damage and subsequent baggage that molestation produces in its victims is immeasurable.

Estimates vary as to the impact molestation has on homosexuality. I have seen research that as many as fifty-eight percent or more of those in the homosexual lifestyle have been sexually abused in their developing years.[7] Others claim this figure is inflated. The fact remains that far too many young girls and boys have been sexually violated, and this clearly contributes to a promiscuous lifestyle, whether heterosexual or homosexual. Of course, pedophilia contributes enormously to this problem.

Parental Adultery

Like spousal abuse, the exposure of a young person to parental adultery is not likely to be the sole determining factor in the boy or girl's eventual attraction to same-sex relationships. It can, however, contribute to the equation, particularly when the adultery is encountered during the volatile adolescent years. It poses even greater problems when the young man or woman actually witnesses the parent taking part in a sexual act. The undermining of trust, the confusion about sexuality, and anger over parental betrayal all play a part in this particular dynamic.

The Mixed Messages of Relativism

When there are no fixed standards or norms, young people do not know right from wrong. And, outside the parameters of religious communities, there are no absolutes to hinder, give guidance, set boundaries, or determine direction (this is not to say that these absolutes aren't violated within faith communities). Beyond most religious guidelines, everything is "relative." Whatever makes a person feel good at the moment becomes the acceptable standard, and in reality, this amounts to no standard at all. Morality (or the lack thereof) is based on each individual's selfish interests and wayward emotions. As George Barna has written:

> Consider the issue of truth. About three-quarters of all adults reject the notion that there are absolute moral truths.

Most Americans believe that all truth is relative to the situation and the individuals involved. Similarly, at least three-quarters of our teens embrace the same position regarding moral truths. Not only do more than three out of four teenagers say there is no absolute moral truth; four out of five also claim that nobody can know for certain whether or not they actually know what truth is. This may also help to explain why a majority of teenagers (57 percent) say that lying is sometimes necessary—not merely convenient, common, understandable or acceptable, but necessary.

Today's youth are likely to describe themselves as moral not because of what they do, but because of how they feel. Because they believe they always try to make the right decision in any situation, most deem themselves to be moral individuals. In practice, however, they live in accordance with situational ethics and moral relativism.[8]

Seduction by Peers

Peer pressure is tremendous at the junior high and high school level. Being "cool" means buying into the idea that "everyone is doing it," and experimenting with homosexuality may be "super cool" in some circles, particularly if alcohol and drugs are involved in removing inhibitions. As young people seek for personal identity and acceptance, being liked is a powerful influence. It significantly shapes who they are and what they will do to feel in with their peers.

Temptation

This is what I call getting "blindsided" and can happen to anyone at any time or place. We as parents can only hope that the foundations for opposing temptation are firm enough in our young people that they will have good judgment and the vitality to stand firm when temptations occur. From my experience and observation comes a warning that we are the most vulnerable to temptation after an emotional high.

In *How Will I Tell My Mother?* Jerry Arterburn, who eventually died of AIDS, writes:

> After speaking on . . . Laymen's Sunday . . . I felt like nothing could compare with the sensation of doing something so significant as that. I was bumping heaven! Afterward the relief set in while the congregation came by and told me I had done a good job. They even made comments to the preacher that he had better watch out or I would replace him. It was a grand evening. One of the members said the nicest thing I ever heard. He said, "I'm glad I know you!"
>
> What happened within the next few hours was in direct contrast with the experience I had at church, but in form it is similar to what happens to many others—ministers and lay people—after a major spiritual victory. I believe many have been led astray in the hours following a wonderful experience with God. Our vulnerability to Satan is the strongest in the hours after a close . . . walk with God.[9]

Jerry goes on to describe that being at the "wrong time at the right place" led to temptation, and ultimately to a life of homosexuality.

Poor Eye-to-Hand Coordination

Not being able to participate well in sports is a personal disaster for many a young man. This is frequently the result of what some have labeled "poor eye-to-hand coordination." It may be because of something as simple as poor vision, or it may stem from improper development of athletic skills in childhood, but when a guy is always picked last for the team, he will probably be called a "sissy," a "fag," or some other name that degrades his masculinity. Men who have become involved in the homosexual lifestyle often cite these early rejections on the playground as the beginning of their problems with sexual identity.

Chemical Imbalances

Because of the complexities of this particular issue, I will defer to George Rekers' indispensable book, *Handbook on Child and Adolescent Sexual Problems*, published by Lexington Books in 1995.[10] Chapter 6 is titled "Psychological Issues in Individuals with Genetic, Hormonal, and Anatomic Anomalies of the Sexual System." This chapter addresses genetic, hormonal, and anatomic anomalies of the reproductive organs, as well as the psychological effects associated with these defects. Also discussed are the medical and psychological treatments for these individuals and their families.

Failure of Leadership

The failure of respected leaders can devastate our youth. Watching a role model crumble because of a moral failure or a lack of integrity can derail young men and women, and some of them never seem to recover from the heartbreak of being let down or betrayed by their model. Those of us in leadership positions know that people following us have the right to expect a higher standard of integrity and character from us. That doesn't mean that we're perfect and never make mistakes, but it does mean that we have to take responsibility for our actions, and must quickly repent if we stumble.

After Sam left, I sat and talked for awhile with Pastor Bob and Carl. I felt grateful to both of them for their support in developing a church program for the prevention of homosexuality.

"You know, the thing that worries me the most is that so few churches seem to be open or receptive to this idea. They may nod and smile, but after a few conversations, it's pretty obvious that they wouldn't touch this issue with a ten-foot pole."

Carl nodded. "I think they're afraid of some kind of a stigma," *he said. "In youth groups, for example, they want to attract all the cool, popular kids. If a bunch of kids they see as misfits start attending, they're afraid it'll drive away all the others and the whole thing will fall apart."*

Pastor Bob agreed, "Adults aren't quite as obvious about that kind of thing, at least not at first. But I don't have to tell you what will happen if homosexual couples start attending our church. There are people who simply won't sit in the same room with them."

"It's not as if you've preached that homosexual behavior is okay with you and okay with God," Carl pointed out. "You've always said it's a sin, but you've also said that Jesus came to save sinners. I haven't seen any gay couples in the sanctuary yet, but I've seen a couple of people I know to be involved in the homosexual lifestyle. They usually come to church by themselves."

Pastor Bob absently took off his glasses and polished them with his tie. "One of them made an appointment to talk to me the other day. His dad's a pastor, and the poor kid is so confused. He thinks he's committed the 'unforgivable sin.' I hope I was able to convince him otherwise. He just tested HIV-positive, and he needs to be in a loving Christian community. I hope our church turns out to be it."

"I'm not sure Sam is going to hang in with us," Carl frowned.

*"Only time will tell," Pastor Bob said. "But I think Sam's got
a battle going on inside him, and I have a feeling the Lord's
going to win it."*

*I shook my head, genuinely worried. "Let's just hope Sam
doesn't lose Jason in the process."*

*We prayed together for Sam and the young man with HIV
and committed ourselves to keep doing battle in prayer on their
behalf daily. We all knew that just learning good principles is
not enough. These friends needed a power beyond that of the
human will—and we knew our Lord would pour out his supernatural strength if we would do our jobs as leaders and continually bring this situation to him in prayer.*

Are We Really "Salt and Light"?

A failure in leadership has to do with more than individuals.
It has to do with the response of the Christian community to
the world. When the Christian church conforms to the
world's value system, it no longer is "salt and light," offering
preservation and guidance to the society around it.

I receive volumes of leadership and management litera-
ture, sent to me by both secular and Christian establish-
ments. If the identifying labels were ripped off and the logos
erased, I would not be able to tell where many of them origi-
nated. They are virtually identical in method and approach,
each seeking to accomplish a similar goal—success at any
cost. They promote doing whatever it takes to get power,
people, or profit.

The message I hear is that the ends really do justify the
means. This can mean using hate and fear to raise money. It
can mean slandering other people or organizations. It can
mean self-righteously passing judgment or falsely accusing

another in order to elevate individuals into positions of authority. It can mean exaggerating about the severity of a situation in order to manipulate emotions.

This raises an interesting question: Has the world become godly, or has the Christian community become worldly? It seems rather obvious to me that the Christian community has become worldly and doesn't even know it.

We rationalize, justify, and spiritualize everything we do by saying that what we are doing is for "God's Kingdom," "The Christian Cause," or "Christ's Ministry in Our Generation." This seems to excuse all kinds of behavior, most notably the way we treat people as "things" to be exploited and used, oftentimes for the financing of "God's" work. Jesus didn't come to launch a fund-raising campaign for himself or for anyone else. Nor did he come to start a "cause" or a "movement." Jesus came to bring people into a complete and abundant relationship with his Father. Our mission should be precisely the same—no more, no less.

Oswald Chambers writes, "Paul was not given a message or a doctrine to proclaim, he was brought into a vivid, personal, overmastering relationship to Jesus Christ. Acts 26:16 is immensely commanding—'to make thee a minister and a witness.' There is nothing there apart from the personal relationship. Paul was devoted to a Person not to a 'cause.' He was absolutely Jesus Christ's, he saw nothing else, he lived for nothing else." [11]

Even the apostle Paul did not put the "ministry" ahead of the colleagues God had given him. In 2 Corinthians 2:12–13 we find Paul in a ministry explosion, faced with an open door given by the Lord—but Titus was nowhere in sight. Paul left what appeared to be the most exceptional ministry opportunity that had ever been available to him. Instead of pursuing it, he went to Macedonia looking for Titus. *Paul did not sacrifice the individual for the big picture of the calling that God had given him. Individuals came first, and the ministry always came second.*

In *America's Only Hope*, Tony Evans writes:

> Rather than the world coming to the church for solutions, the church begs the world for solutions. For example, the church has often surrendered its rightful agenda to political programs. It has hopped on the backs of donkeys and elephants, hoping they will provide solutions to society's problems. The black church often depends on the Democratic Party and its quest for social justice. The white church often depends on the Republican Party in its quest for morality. Neither church fully realizes that no political party fully functions according to God's agenda.
>
> We have allowed ourselves to become so mixed up with the world's agenda, standards, and methodologies that we have lost our identity as God's people. Because the church can't get its own house in order, it has very little to say to the broader society. Plagued with moral and financial scandals and rebellious and ungodly leaders, the church's pale effectiveness is overlooked by the world. It's a direct result of the church's failure to commit itself to God's agenda.[12]

In the United States, our money bears the imprint, "In God we trust." We have church buildings on every corner. We have Christian books on just about any subject, along with Christian tapes, Christian videos, Christian music, Christian conference grounds, Christian education from preschool through graduate institutions, Christian radio programs, and a host of Christian TV shows.

For where jealousy and selfish ambition exist, there is disorder and every evil thing. (James 3:16, NASB)

Yet, rather than being identified with the life and person of Jesus Christ, Christians are identified with political extremism, money scandals, sexual disgrace, bigotry, conspiracy theories, and a subculture that operates with a bunker mentality. In my lifetime, pastors used to be the most respected people in the community. The church building was a place of respect, held in reverence. One naturally expected an "honest deal" if the person was identified with the local body of Christian believers.

What's happened? Is it society's fault? Or does the church need to point a finger at itself? Have we failed to reveal true Christianity to the ones who should be coming to know Christ, but cannot seem to find any trace of him, not even in our churches?

Is it any wonder that young people who are struggling with gender confusion run away from our picture-perfect, image-conscious youth groups? As Carl pointed out in our story, we seem to be more concerned with keeping the "numbers" up, with making things "seeker-friendly," with conforming to the socially acceptable norms, than with reaching out to the confused, the unattractive, the socially challenged (and challenging), the "strange" in style, or the "extreme" in behavior.

"The only thing dirtier than being a lesbian in a Christian community is being a Christian in a lesbian community."
—Kathleen Boatwright
The gay subculture teems with hostility toward religion and in particular toward Christianity. . . . Many homosexuals

179

were rejected by their parents in the name of Christianity. . . .
To such homosexuals the church represents not a foundation
for love and hope, but a memory of hatred and rejection.
—Bruce Bawer[13]

When Jesus stood before Pilate, Pilate asked, "What is truth?" I think he was really saying, "There is no such thing as truth. And who cares about truth, anyway? We Romans are interested in building empires, in efficiency and financial stability, and in conquering the world. Truth? You've got to be kidding!"

And what about today? Is truth an important issue in our modern society? The last several years have given us some insight into ourselves. We have placed in leadership not those who stand for truth and integrity, but those who are telegenic, who have projected the "right" image, and who offer us financial betterment.

Maybe we Christians are no different from Pilate and from the Romans in Jesus' time. We are very affluent, but doesn't "moral poverty" also describe us?

What about Sodom and Gomorrah?

Those who most loudly attack homosexuals often cite the biblical account of Sodom and Gomorrah, which begins in Genesis 13. There are, however, some interesting insights to be found in the story having to do with Abraham's nephew Lot, who became a citizen of Sodom in high standing, and a series of choices he made. Even though the New Testament calls Lot a "righteous man" (2 Peter 2:7), if we take a close look, I believe you will agree with me that the overriding theme of Lot's life was one of self-promotion and compromise. I also think we may see some disappointing contrasts between Abraham's response to wrongdoing and that of our own Christian community.

In Genesis 12, I read that Abraham adopted and raised his nephew Lot. This gave Lot the opportunity to watch his uncle's walk with God. In seeing this, he doubtless observed both the highs and lows of his uncle's spiritual pilgrimage. He probably witnessed how God dealt with Abraham when he told the half lie about Sarah, his wife. Most likely, Lot was present during the confrontation between Pharaoh and Abraham. And he also would have experienced, firsthand, Abraham's sincere worship of the living God.

In Genesis 13, we come to the problem of material blessing called "overabundance of wealth"—too many cattle for the land to bear. Even though, by custom and family position, Abraham had the first choice of whatever land he wanted, he gave that up, deferring to Lot to make the call between a beautiful, fertile, lush valley and a rough hillside. Lot chose the lush valley, and in that valley stood the cities of Sodom and Gomorrah. Now, let's think this through.

First, Lot really owed all his wealth and success to his Uncle Abraham.

Second, in the choice he made, he showed no respect for his uncle or gratitude for Abraham's role in raising him.

Nevertheless, it is not difficult to imagine Lot's thinking: "If I am going to continue to prosper, I'll need the lush valley. The arid land in the other direction can't compare with the grasslands. The cities will give my family some social opportunities, and the children will definitely benefit from the better quality of life in the city. They'll have a better chance at a good education. And who knows, maybe with my successful background, I'll have some political clout and influence."

So Lot moved toward Sodom. He didn't exactly settle

there, but in very close proximity. By chapter 14, however, Lot was living in Sodom, and Uncle Abraham had to come to his rescue. It seems that Lot and his family were taken hostage during a local military conflict, kidnapped from their homes, and taken to a foreign place.

Now here's an interesting question. How would Abraham view Lot's situation if he were a participant in today's church society? Maybe he would say . . .

- Serves him right, he didn't give me the respect that I earned.

- Lot messed up his own life—I warned him, but did he listen to me?

- Why should I put all my possessions at risk trying to bail him out?

- My whole life and the life of my family could be drastically affected if I get involved.

- Lot probably has AIDS anyway, living around those people.

In fact, Abraham didn't say anything of the kind. He didn't say anything at all, as far as I know. He simply risked his life to save his wayward nephew.

The Bible describes Lot "sitting in the gate of Sodom." Scholars believe this may indicate that Lot was the mayor or some other high official of Sodom. He apparently had made it to the top, politically speaking. In Genesis 18, Abraham is attempting to make a bargain with God over the destruction of Sodom and Gomorrah. He has been warned that God is about to destroy the city for its wickedness, and Abraham asks God if he will spare the city if he can find fifty righteous people living there. Abraham continues the bargaining until he gets God down to the number ten. A question runs through my mind: why did he stop at ten? Maybe if Lot had been a good spiritual leader of his family, ten would have been enough. Here's how I add up his situation:

Gen. 19:12: sons is used in the plural—so at least	2
19:14: sons-in-law who married daughters—plural again	4
19:15: two unmarried daughters	2
Lot and his wife	2
Total	10

If my calculations are correct, and if Lot had influenced his extended family for God, Sodom would have been saved and not destroyed. But Lot always seemed to have other things on his mind—the very same things that made him choose the lush valley in the first place: comfort, affluence, prestige, and success.

The question that needs to be asked of our Christian community is do we identify more with Abraham or with Lot? And how does God see us, more like Abraham or more like Lot?

It's really no wonder our culture and society reject our message. It's no wonder they want nothing to do with us. Why should the world take us seriously?

Conservative churches, which pay as much lip service to Christian charity as anybody else, are rendered particularly vulnerable by the callous hypocrisy regarding AIDS sufferers. —Marshall Kirk and Hunter Madsen[14]

We tell ourselves we are building those buildings, developing these massive companies and organizations for Jesus, but are they really shrines for him or for us? My observation over the years is that we are more interested in "sheep counting and corralling" than in getting involved with caring for sick, wounded sheep or in cleaning up the manure they leave in the corrals. We think that's for someone else to do—not us.

Since I am focusing on the issue of homosexuality—forgive my bluntness—but why have so few in the Christian community gotten involved in hospice work or in caring for those who are dying with AIDS? Why do our youth ministries ostracize gender-confused young men and women when the church may be their last stop before they turn to the homosexual community for refuge? Why are homosexuals so unwelcome in our churches, when we claim to have the message of life that could save their souls, and maybe their lives?

We certainly didn't learn this kind of ostracization from Jesus. In one very specific example, he offered *honor and respect* to someone who was deemed socially unacceptable, particularly by the faith community of his day. In John 4:4–42, we read of his encounter with the woman of Samaria. Historically, we know that the Jews would rather go around Samaria than travel through it. Maybe this was racism or maybe it was simply bad blood between the people. Whatever the problem was, Jesus placed himself in a vulnerable position by being in hostile territory. He also broke tradition as a man by addressing a woman. He further broke tradition by asking a favor of her; in fact, she was somewhat taken aback by it. He energetically involved himself in his conversation with her, thus identifying her as a person loved by God. Jesus did all this even though he knew all about the woman's unsavory life story. As a result, the whole city was attracted to Jesus by the woman's testimony of her encounter with him.

Every Christian minister in a position of pastoral responsibility needs to ask himself or herself how far their congregation or fellowship is known to respond in a positive, helpful and caring way to homosexuals. Those who suggest that the question has not yet arisen—"we don't have that sort of person here"—may well be unaware of the needs in their midst. —Elizabeth Moberly[15]

The Jesus I know also touched lepers, who were the outcasts of his day. He didn't send his disciples to do it or give them a few coins to distribute among the afflicted. Jesus touched them himself, despite their unclean status, and met them at their point of need. He dined with the despised tax collectors. He was accused of hanging out with prostitutes and other notorious sinners. Should we do less? Or should we say, "They brought it on themselves," and walk away?

Of course there are exceptions to the rule that Christians don't reach out to untouchables. Both here and abroad, Diana and I have met men and women whose feet we don't even feel adequate to wash. These have given their life's blood in the name of Jesus to the poor, wounded, destitute, and rejected of society. We personally know:

- Workers who care for those dying with AIDS, changing their diapers, and in the end burying them. Many of those victims' families have rejected them and denied they ever existed.

- Workers and caretakers who help care for abused women and children.

- Workers who tenderly care for those who are addicted to drugs and alcohol.

- Providers who help the homeless find jobs and shelters.

- Providers who furnish medical care and assistance to those who cannot afford it.

- Providers of assistance and training for those living in slums. We have personally visited these in Latin America, Africa, Philippines, India, and China.

- Pastors and lay workers going into war torn countries to give assistance, many times dodging bullets and antiaircraft fire.

- Young professionals who take their professions into "hostile" countries, placing themselves and their families at risk of their lives.

In his day Jesus said that the fields were white unto harvest, but the laborers were few. Sadly, this is as true today as it was then. Our hats are off to those who are risking life and limb for the sake of God's Kingdom.

Recently, we came in contact with a group of earnest and committed youth pastors who deeply desire to make a difference in the lives of youth who struggle with gender identity. These women and men are seeking ways to reach out to boys and girls who manifest some of the "warning signs" we listed in chapter 1. These youth leaders have begun to implement some practical actions intended to turn the tide in young people's lives before they begin to act out sexually. Here are the action steps they are taking:

Twelve Positive Action Steps
All of the following must be handled tactfully and without a dramatic shift in interaction with the young person. These are usually very sensitive and intuitive individuals who will find overt attempts at "changing" them all too obvious and censorious.
1. Do everything in light of God's Word and God's love. A group lesson on biblical views of homosexual behavior, including facts and falsehoods surrounding the subject, and a forthright discussion addressing the stigma attached to the issue would be a logical place to begin. There is a remarkable amount of fear associated with this subject, especially among adolescent males. It is a topic that inspires relentless ridicule, locker room humor, and unapologetic prejudice.

The challenge is to find a way to overcome these reactions and replace them with an inclusive, instead of exclusive, environment for all young no matter what their difficulties. This objective becomes more complex if the adults involved are struggling with their own fears and insecurities on the subject.

Christian love is the ultimate goal. And teaching young people to love the "unlovable" is a key life lesson, no matter what makes the outsider less appealing than the average boy or girl. It must be communicated that reaching out to "at-risk" kids is just one more opportunity to demonstrate the unconditional—and tough—love of Jesus to those who need him the most. If young people can catch that vision and set aside their homophobia, the process will be immeasurably easier. One way of addressing this is to compare homosexual behavior with smoking or with drug or alcohol abuse—we continue to be a friend to the person involved, but we clearly let him or her know that we cannot approve of or participate in their self-destructive behavior.

2. Be inclusive no matter what. It is essential that both youth leaders and young people suppress their inclination to avoid him or her. Instead, include him/her in all activities, especially sports for boys (try to avoid situations where he or she is the last one picked for teams).

3. Introduce positive role models. Provide healthy same-sex heterosexual role models for the at-risk boys and girls. A healthy family environment, strong male leadership, and appropriate female behavior all contribute to a healthy socialization process.

4. Reinforce true sexual identity. Affirmation of the whole person, his or her accomplishments, appearance, and sexually appropriate behavior can rebuild the broken places in a young person's heart and soul. Remember how very insecure this boy or girl is on the inside and how he or she craves attention and applause.

5. Find a way to address abuse. Seek, if possible, to identify molestation/abuse issues, and find godly counsel for him/her. Be sure any counselors involved have a biblical and informed view of homosexuality, not assuming it to be "genetically predetermined."

6. Note possible hormonal problems. Sometimes extreme cross-gender behavior is the result of hormonal imbalances and can be successfully treated by a qualified physician. If you suspect this may be the case, try to raise the issue with the young person's parents and suggest a medical evaluation.

7. Communicate! Work to establish dialogue. Listen carefully, and be informed enough to answer questions that arise.

8. Applaud every positive effort. Reinforce any and all efforts and evidence of change. This young person is emerging from a deception—make sure the truth is reaffirmed often and enthusiastically.

9. Teach the Bible. Both the youth group and each individual young person should be well taught about Christian principles regarding homosexuality, chastity, forgiveness, thought control, and being "transformed by the renewing of your mind."

10. Confront carefully, if at all. Do not confront without agreement between youth workers, pastors, and Christian counselors, taking into consideration the anticipated family response. If confrontation is to be made, do so with wisdom, discretion, and prayer. And whatever you do, don't accuse!

11. Encourage openness. Allow emotional release, and don't be surprised by an intense outpouring of feelings and fears. If a professional counselor seems appropriate, find a way to make this possible, taking into consideration finances, transportation, and family concerns.

This does not mean, by the way, that you should be subjected to an endless recital of problems or an airing of "dirty laundry." A "talk show" approach can cause a person's wrong behavior to become the center of attention and can perversely reward bad actions. Instead, listen for awhile, then provide a positive suggestion or two, and ask the person to report back to you how the suggestions worked out. Above all else, let the person know you genuinely care about him or her.

12. Prepare for honest disclosure. If the boy or girl raises the issues or identifies homosexual concerns, along with the above steps, use this problem-solving model:

Evaluate the situation prayerfully.
Determine the real problem.
Establish accountability.
Select a plan of action.
List alternative solutions.

In my experience, gender issues in a youth group setting generally should not be confrontational unless leadership agrees that it is appropriate. Instead, the Twelve Action Steps can be applied without directly addressing the possibility of a young person's tendencies toward homosexuality. Confrontation may be unwise unless a young person brings it up and seeks help or unless the adults involved conclude, preferably with the advice of a qualified Christian counselor, that it is the best way to resolve an issue. In any case, accusation should be explicitly avoided.

Solidarity with families is an important principle. It would be ideal if the young person's family could be brought into the picture, informed, and encouraged to seek help for their son or daughter. But unfortunately, the youngsters who need parental support and assistance the very most are often the ones least likely to receive it. A deeply troubled home life is all too frequently a key element in homosexual behavior.

Parents may become unduly alarmed—even hostile—if the issue of homosexuality is raised, especially if it involves their own children. This is particularly true if they are not supportive of Bible-based values, feel personally threatened by the subject, are socially involved in homosexuality themselves, or have a critical attitude toward the youth group leadership. Clearly, this is a highly sensitive concern that can create exceptionally defensive reactions if not handled wisely.

Sam called me at eleven on a Friday night, just as I was falling asleep. He was in a frenzy. "Don, you should see the little queer Jason brought home for dinner tonight. I can't believe my eyes! As far as I'm concerned, you and Carl are dead wrong about him, and this proves it."

Next morning, bright and early, I drove over to the church, where I had agreed to meet with Carl, Sam, and Jason. I wasn't exactly looking forward to the confrontation, but it was time we all discussed Jason's situation openly.

Jason, who was dressed in black, sat slumped in his seat with a surly look on his face. He seemed to be staring at a spot on the wall.

Sam was pale and drawn and looked as if he hadn't slept all night. He was staring at Jason.

Carl, who seemed perfectly comfortable, said a very surprising thing. "Jason, I'm not sure why we're getting together this morning. But before we get started, I want to thank you for taking Stephen under your wing last night. He's really in need of some friends. You may have noticed that he's very confused."

Jason laughed out loud, "He's confused all right. He says he wants to try heroin, he's already tried crack, he thinks he's an alcoholic, and he's almost sure he's bisexual. Now that's what I call confused!"

"Well, just taking him to your home was a really generous thing. Thanks to you, too, Sam, for making him welcome. We're all trying to learn how to reach out to some pretty messed up kids, and we're going to need all the help we can find."

I looked at Sam, and Sam looked at me. I said, "Sam, maybe we need to tell you a little more about the program we're working on. If you're interested, you can play an important role in it, because Jason's agreed to participate. Do you want to know more?"

Sam sighed, and for once I think he really felt as if a load had been taken off his back. He spent a minute or two thinking through the situation and trying to absorb a whole new set of facts. Finally he spoke, and I felt a surge of hope that his words might well be marking the beginning of a new relationship with his son.

"Jason," he said, "if you want to do some kind of ministry, I'd like to help. Maybe it's something we can work on together . . ."

"Maybe so, Dad."

It wasn't easy. It wasn't always pleasant or fun. But that's exactly what they did.

Chapter Nine

Forgiveness and
Peace of Mind

Throughout the pages of this book, we have examined many situations that can, in myriad combinations, set the stage for same-sex attraction, or a homosexual condition or lifestyle. Your response thus far to these issues will probably have depended on the role you play. You may be a parent. You may be a youth worker. You may be a pastor. You may be a young person confused about gender. Or you may have concluded that you are a homosexual.

It bears repeating—whoever you are and whatever you have experienced, the message I hear from those who wrestle with the issue of homosexuality is that you are clearly in tremendous emotional pain. The second distinct message I hear is that you long for inner peace: those closest to this explosive and divisive issue seem to have the least peace.

God has made some wonderful promises about inner peace, and we'll look at them in a moment. But for now, let's consider the number one reason we humans, Christian or non-Christian, lack peace. That reason has to do with disobedience and unforgiveness. Either we have wronged others and have not sought their forgiveness. Or perhaps more commonly, we have unforgiveness in our hearts toward those who have wronged us, toward ourselves, or toward God.

Sometimes we use our anger as fuel. Sometimes we keep bitterness inside, hoping that those who have wronged us will "pay." Sometimes we don't even realize we have an unforgiving spirit. Maybe we can't get past a painful memory. Perhaps we can't wish the best for someone who hurt us. Or we may simply find ourselves rejoicing at the suffering of an enemy. The greatest clue, of course, is when we hear ourselves saying, "I'll never forgive that person as long as I live!" Or we shake our heads and sigh, "That was simply unforgivable."

Refusing to Forgive

Why do we refuse to forgive others? Sometimes we find it difficult to forgive someone because of the level of wrong we have suffered and the pain it has cost us. But that isn't the only reason. It isn't unusual for our own self-righteousness to get in the way of our willingness to forgive. These two dynamics combine into a position that could be verbalized like this, "How could he do that to me? I would never do such a terrible thing!" This is particularly common in situations that relate to sexual misconduct, whether homosexual or heterosexual.

For if you forgive men when they sin against you, your heavenly Father will also forgive you.(Matthew 6:14)

In my teen years, a number of male mentors had a positive influence in my life. One mentor in particular made a very significant impact on me. But after I had known him—closely—for a few years, he did something that was very ungodly and, to my view, despicable. Although he truly repented and reconciled himself to the hurt parties in an honorable fashion, in my immaturity and self-righteousness, I couldn't forgive him. I had lost all respect for the man.

Well, I believe God has a sense of humor, and so I sometimes think devises very creative ways for getting my attention. One summer, my wife and I went on a camping trip in the mountains, and when we arrived at the campground, we found out there was only one campsite left. And guess who "just happened" to be camped right next to us? You guessed it—my ex-mentor.

I still thought the man was quite unworthy, but I reluctantly condescended to put on a friendly face and be pleasant to him (as pleasant as a "more righteous" man could possibly be). To my discomfort, Diana and I were invited to join them around their campfire that evening. It wasn't long before he and I were face to face, alone. Trying to be a good actor, I continued to wear my insincere smile.

The "fallen" man, who was being far more sincere than I was, began to open up about his sin and the ramifications of his actions. With shining eyes, he told me how God had redirected his life's ministry. He explained how he was now working with the hurting people of our society, and he was looking forward to retirement so he could devote even more time and energy to this new ministry.

God had hit me with his proverbial sledgehammer. I could all but hear him say to me, "Don, how can you refuse to forgive and reconcile yourself to my servant? He has repented, he has dealt honorably with the consequences of his sin, and he is enthusiastically moving forward in my service. Who made you his judge?"

Of course I did forgive him. In fact, I needed to ask his forgiveness for my self-righteous attitude toward him. As a result, I have a restored mentor, one whom I hold in the highest esteem.

Forgiving "Those Who Trespass against Us"

Sometimes forgiving those who have hurt us is easier said than done. I have been closely involved with two separate situations, trying to help victims deal with inflicted pain. The first one turned out quite well—at least as well as could be expected. The second was disastrous. First, let's invite "Elise" to tell her story for herself. This is a real letter from a real teenager. It is her response to her father's "coming out," written in her own words.

> "Kids, I'm a homosexual." Suddenly, the "rock" upon which I had built my life gave way. My life came crashing down around me.
>
> In an instant, my father fell from the pedestal upon which I had placed him. "How could you be a homosexual, Dad? After seventeen years of marriage, you just decide you're gay?"
>
> How would my friends react? How could we be seen in public? Could I ever look him in the eye with the same love and affection as before? Was this the same man who comforted me when I was down and kissed me at night when he tucked me into bed? Was loving him something I could do again?
>
> Devastated, I struggled to grasp for answers to questions

that previously didn't exist. My mom thought counseling was the answer. "It'll help you sort things out," she advised. "It'll help you feel like I'm sorting them out," I retorted angrily. Grief stricken, I sought the advice of a counselor and asked God to help me rebuild the relationship with my dad. Embarking on this journey is the hardest thing I have ever done.

Overcoming the disillusionment has been the greatest obstacle. Gradually, I am learning to love my dad again, even though I still struggle with his lifestyle. Although disappointed, I am persevering, learning to be a more confident, caring person, and constantly trying to love people for who they are, not what they do.

Then Peter came to Jesus and asked, "Lord, how many times shall I forgive my brother when he sins against me? Up to seven times?" Jesus answered, "I tell you, not seven times, but seventy times seven." (Matthew 18:21–22)

The second story is a heartbreaker. "Lynne" is a very beautiful young lady, who was raised in what she has described as a Christian home. In fact, her father is the pastor of a church. But while working through her life's struggles in counseling, Lynne finally admitted that her father had sexually molested her over a period of years in the developing stage of her life.

Since this man was both Lynne's father and the spiritual head of her church, she was profoundly wounded. Her father's sexual deviation and double life has corrupted her view of God as Heavenly Father.

At the counselor's insistence, Lynne finally got up the courage to confront Pastor Dad about the past. The man neither denied his actions, nor took responsibility for them. He simply said, "God has forgiven me, and you have to forgive me too." What a brutal response from a victimizer who is doubly responsible to God as a man in a position of spiritual authority! How could Lynne possibly reply?

As it turned out, she has responded in the worst way possible. She has become extremely promiscuous, devious, and dishonest, and she is struggling with overpowering, life-threatening addictions. The "what ifs" in Lynne's tragic story go on and on. What if Lynne's father had repented and asked her forgiveness, assuring her of his remorse? What if he had confessed his sin? What if she had found the spiritual strength to see him as he is and to rise above his abuses? What if she'd found it in her soul to forgive him, while still holding him responsible for his wrongdoing?

Those questions, at least for now, will never be answered. Instead of humbling himself and confessing his fault, this man—who continues to preach and carry out the role of a senior pastor—refuses to affirm his daughter, to accept her, or to admit to his enormous wrongdoing. Today, Lynne is caught in a web of evil and danger from which only God will be able to deliver her.

Both Lynne and Elise were terribly wounded by their fathers' behavior. And they both were faced with the task of forgiveness when it seemed impossible to them. This raises a profound question: How are we expected to forgive, when those who have hurt us refuse to repent and confess? Our example, of course, is Jesus. While he suffered the worst injustice of all—dying in complete innocence at the hand of evildoers—he verbally forgave those who were killing him. His murderers did not repent, and he forgave them anyway.

"Sure, but he was God," we say. True, but Jesus was fully human too. Forgiving the unrepentant isn't easy. It doesn't feel right or fair. Without counsel and prayer, it may be impossible. But can we do less than try to follow the example of our Lord?

How Do We Get beyond the Rage?

Forgiveness can seem like an insurmountable barrier in our lives. And the degree of difficulty isn't necessarily equivalent to the degree of wrong we've suffered. Sometimes in life I have found it easy to forgive huge offenses while I've struggled with lesser ones. Many years ago, our family was embroiled in a financial crisis. In fact we were somewhere in the middle of an eight-year period during which our farming operation provided no support for us at all. Diana was working at a job in town to keep the four of us afloat financially. On the bright side, however, we were having good success with a Christian university ministry.

One day another campus minister, who was working at the same university, approached me to form what he called a "united, cooperative-operative relationship." He explained that this would present to the students a "oneness in Christ" between his ministry and ours. That sounded great to us, and we gave him our wholehearted support.

Diana and I failed to see the man's hidden agenda. Our ministry happened to have a very good balance between male and female students. But before we knew it, the male student leaders, whom I had spent several years training, left my leadership to join the other man in his "greater vision" for the campus. Diana and I were left with only women students, and for all practical purposes, this shut down our work. In those days, men would not attend a religious group that had a large constituency of females.

I was enraged. I felt that I had been betrayed by a Christian brother in the ministry, and even though I tried to forgive and reconcile with him, bitterness was eating me alive. I had moments of feeling that I had successfully overcome my anger, but the next thing I knew a raging war was going on inside me again. It was even beginning to affect my health.

The pain I suffered at this man's hand could not be compared to that of Elise or Lynne. In fact, I can name several worse situations in my own experience, where forgiveness came easily and spontaneously. But whatever the size of the "trespass," my conflict was monumental.

Fortunately, my friends and family were praying for me, and God was very gently communicating with me. He tried to remind me that my ministry was really his ministry—at least that was what I had been saying all along. Nonetheless, my usual method of verbal forgiveness and a subsequent attempt to be cordial and friendly weren't working this time. I was so controlled by my anger that I could hardly live with myself. Come to think of it, I'm not sure how Diana and the rest of our ministry team managed to live with me either.

Unwelcome Words from Heaven

It wasn't long before I was reminded (again) that we serve a faithful and ingenious God, who was about to expose me to some very practical steps for forgiveness. I had been doing my daily quiet time in the gospel of Luke. One morning I came across something I viewed as a totally unreasonable, unthinkable, and radical approach to dealing with personal injustice. My comment at the time was, "God, you've got to be kidding. No way!"

That morning's meditation was Luke 6:27–30, which I quote from the King James Version in which I read it:

> "But I say unto you which hear, Love your enemies, do good to them which hate you, Bless them that curse you, and pray for them which despitefully use you. And unto him that smiteth thee on the one cheek offer also the other; and him that taketh away thy cloak forbid not to take thy coat also. Give to every man that asketh of thee; and of him that taketh away thy goods ask them not again."

- Love your enemies. Well, I thought this was a little radical, but Jesus was a radical sort of a guy, and it fit his style.

- Do good to those who hate you. That took me a step further, and I didn't particularly like the idea of doing anything good for my adversary.

- Bless those who curse you. That was even more ridiculous. What human in his right mind would do that?

- Pray for those who mistreat you. Now just a minute. Was God saying that I should ask him to bless that man and his ministry? His ministry that used to be *my ministry?* Forget it! I flatly refused.

I searched for a more liberal translation of the passage, but to my horror, they all seemed to say the same thing. In fact, some were even more direct. And as I reflected on this passage, I couldn't help but wonder if Jesus was really serious in what he said. I could buy the "love your enemies" bit in theory, but it seemed to me that he was telling me exactly how he wanted it done. And I didn't like it.

God and I sparred for several days. I was having the worst time of my life, stubbornly refusing to obey. I came up with all the reasons I could muster about why God was wrong about this one. But God is patient and persistent. He never backed off or changed his mind, despite my reasons, rationalizations, and rampages. And, at last, I was able to settle it with him. My prayer sounded something like this.

"O.K., God, you win. You said it, and you must have meant what you said. And I'm going to be perfectly honest with you. I'll do it your way, just out of obedience to your Word, but I have absolutely no good feelings toward that guy. None at all. You told me to, so I'll go ahead and ask you to bless his ministry. And I guess you want me to pray for him every time I get those angry feelings inside. So I'll do it. But I sure don't feel like it."

Well, there was no magical resolution. The campus leader did not repent or seek to reconcile with me for what he had done. In that regard, nothing changed at all. But, something else happened, and it was far more important. Supernaturally (and it had to be supernatural), I found myself with inner peace and the freedom from anger that I had really longed for.

Now I must confess, it didn't happen overnight. But whenever I started feeling the tide of anger rising again, that was my signal from God to pray positively and urgently for this campus leader's student ministry. Sure enough, the rage abated. I became really satisfied with my newly discovered serenity, and righting the wrongs against me didn't matter to me anymore. Experiencing the peace of God was rewarding enough, and I was completely satisfied with the outcome. And what about our ministry? It took a complete team effort to rebuild it, but God ultimately blessed in that endeavor too.

I see many situations in the course of biblical counseling where people need to peel off the layers of insulation that have grown on top of each other, over years of self-protection. The removal of a person's defenses is necessary before either confrontation or forgiveness can be accomplished, and this may even require professional help. But I want to encourage you to begin taking the necessary steps toward forgiveness. I know countless people, who battle all sorts of addictive behaviors, who have experienced growth and deliverance through the forgiveness process.

> *"Forgiveness is not a benefit I bestow on someone else.*
> *It's a freedom I give to myself."*
> —Tony Campbell, quoted in Together Journal

If the offender is dead, unapproachable, or unavailable physically or mentally, you may need to write a letter. After all the past hurts have been written down and signed, I suggest that a little ceremony is held, a prayer offered, and the letter burned. You may need to go through the death process, once you've confronted the loss, so don't be surprised if you experience some grief.

In what we sometimes call the Lord's Prayer, Jesus taught us to say, "And forgive us our trespasses, as we forgive those who trespass against us." We are to forgive as our Heavenly Father has forgiven us. Now for a person who claims Jesus as Lord and Savior, these are very strong words. They seem to be saying that God's forgiveness of us is contingent upon our forgiveness of others.

Fortunately, as I learned, God doesn't expect us to do the impossible. When we pray, we access his life-changing power which is able to heal us and give us the ability to forgive beyond what we could do with just our own will power and desire to do right. This applies when we need to forgive others, and it also applies when we need to forgive ourselves.

Confession and Repentance

Sometimes, of course, we are the wrongdoers. Sometimes we are the ones who have to confess and repent. As we consider the importance of forgiveness, we need to keep in mind that there is a world of difference between superficially saying "I'm sorry" and genuinely repenting for our sinful behavior. This is made clear in Luke 19:8, where Jesus meets up with a fellow named Zaccheus, who had made a very comfortable living by stealing from the local taxpayers. He said, "Behold, Lord, half of my possessions I will give to the poor, and if I have defrauded anyone of anything, I will give back four times as much" (NASB).

Making restitution for our misdeeds is critical. In today's culture, saying "I'm sorry" can be a flippant, socially correct cop-out. But making every effort to right a wrong by making restitution indicates real repentance. Jesus and the Scriptures always describe true repentance in these terms.

Charles Stanley writes, "To repent means to 'change your mind and behavior.' Repentance is an act of the will. It involves follow-through behavior. Confession is an admission; it is saying, 'I have sinned.' Repentance takes that confession and puts it into action. It is declaring, 'I am changing my mind and my behavior so that I will not sin again.' Repentance involves the actual doing of what we say we are going to do

. . . Genuine repentance—the desire and action not to sin again—validates confession. The two are inseparable for any person who desires to walk in close fellowship with God." [1]

"God—I'll Never Forgive You!"

One of the most familiar forms of unforgiveness often slips by us, because we don't see it for what it is. It is incorrect to say that we need to forgive God—God is holy and righteous, and he is incapable of wrongdoing. But in our human ignorance, frustration, and heartbreak, we often blame fate, bad luck, chance, or even some vague, impersonal force we call "Providence" for our problems.

Those of us who believe in a personal and eminent God have to consider just exactly what we mean when we blame external forces for our circumstances. Scratch below the surface, and we hear some agonizing questions:

- Where was God?
- Why didn't he protect my child?
- Why did he allow sexual molestation to happen?
- Couldn't an all-powerful God protect me from an abusive spouse?
- Couldn't God have kept me from marrying a woman like that?
- If God didn't want me to be a homosexual, why did he make me this way?
- If God doesn't want me to sin, can't he stop me?
- If Christians are God's people, why doesn't he make them more loving?

Most Christians believe that God's hand is powerful and mighty and that there are no second causes in our lives—he is responsible for the care and keeping of his adopted children. So what are we supposed to think when things go wrong? When the worst-case scenario happens? When evil seems to prevail?

My own walk with God has forced me to face some of these questions. Although my personal journey did not involve the issue of homosexuality, it certainly did involve a series of painful "accidents" that left me forever damaged. And, like many others who have had to come to terms with the unjust, the unfair, and the unforeseen, I've had to accept God's sovereignty in some very difficult straits.

- An automobile accident, which took place while I was still in high school, was caused by a careless driver who rear-ended my pickup. My boss had no interest in my injuries and sent me back to the produce fields to work with a neck trauma. My neck never really healed and still causes me severe pain, almost half a century later.

- After the birth of our first son Dean, I was praying and thanking God for what seemed to be a very healthy child. Then God asked me a very strange question: "Don, you committed Dean to me before he was born, and now I have given you a son. Just who does he belong to now?" I surrendered Dean back to God, and at that very moment, Dean died while being held in a nurse's arms. I was telephoned to return to the hospital, where I was told, "Your son is dead—what do you want to do with the body? Also, you'll have to be here early in the morning to let your wife know when she wakes up."

- When I was thirty-one, another freak accident took place. A 130-pound bale of hay landed squarely on top of my body, with my pelvis and lower back taking the full blow. Because of financial constraints, I went back to work later that same day and didn't see a doctor until a month of agonizing pain forced me to go. An X-ray showed that my bottom vertebra was completely cracked through the middle, and several bone fragments had chipped off. The doctor didn't mince words. He told me that if I were to stumble, slip, or fall, I would live the rest of my life in a wheelchair. The good news was that I could still walk. The worst news of all was that I had no money or insurance and needed to continue earning a living to support my family. After reviewing my situation, the doctor advised me to "grit my teeth" and bear the pain. He explained that if he were to operate on my back, he would have to give me a fifty-fifty chance of coming out worse off than I already was.

- Being a good environmentalist farmer, I used organic fertilizer. Over the course of twenty years, and without my knowledge, I contacted a very deadly poison from this substance. This poison attacks the nerve endings and causes the muscles to spasm continuously. Fortunately, a doctor whose expertise was in toxins took a special interest in me. He checked with other experts worldwide to find out if there was a cure or antidote for my condition. His report back to me was negative, there is no antidote. He went on to say that the other doctors could not understand why I had not yet died.

- I experienced severe migraine headaches. One episode lasted for three months before a specialist combined five different drugs and stopped the pain. We found out later that those drugs cannot be combined without fatal consequences. During that ordeal, the greatest pain came from a close friend who said, "Don, if you would just confess sin in your life, you wouldn't have these problems." I told him I had confessed all the sin I could think of. I'd asked God to reveal any secret sins. In fact, I even made up some that sounded bad, hoping that would make a difference. My friend still insisted, "You must be hiding something to have these kinds of problems."

Along with a damaged neck, a broken back, and headaches that would not go away, we had severe financial problems, and when we found ourselves $25,000 in debt in one year's farming, I hit a real low. The continuous pain and headaches were getting to me. On top of that I did a little calculation and figured in about a year or so I would probably become a "vegetable," of no profit or help to my family. I really hate to admit this, but suicide crossed my mind.

At about this time, God revealed something to me. "Don, when disaster strikes you unexpectedly, you handle it quite well. But now, when you feel like you're being taken out inch by inch, you have a problem. And the problem is with me."

My reply to God was surprising, even to me. "Okay, God, if allowing me to come to nothing, and if my becoming a burden to my family will bring honor to your name, you have my permission to do it. Your will be done."

From that moment on, an amazing series of events began to unfold. Within two weeks we had two farmers bidding against each other to buy our farm, which we had not been able to sell for ten years. Meanwhile, I came across some Chinese herbs that brought the effects of the poisons under control. I also found a chiropractor who took a very special interest in my case, and over a number of years got me back on my feet, functioning at a respectable pace.

Three lessons became clear throughout the course of all this:

1. Life is not always easy, nor is it particularly fair.
2. God has the right to do with us whatever he chooses.
3. Jesus understands and identifies with us.

Jesus himself experienced the worst injustice possible when Pilate said, "I find no fault in him . . . Crucify him!" (John 19:4, 6, KJV).

When Stephen was being stoned to death, as recorded in Acts 7:55–56, Jesus was "standing at the right hand of God." In Scripture, Jesus is always pictured as sitting at God's right hand. But here we see Jesus standing at attention during Stephen's ordeal, gravely concerned with what was going on with his loyal servant.

Jesus tried to tell us that, at times, his ways might seem unfair to us. We might see him like the friend in Luke 11:5–9, who didn't provide bread when it was needed. Or we might see him like the judge in Luke 18:1–8, who refused to protect the widow. When things get really tough will he find that our faith is still strong?

It is unreasonable for me to blame God for what he does and for what he doesn't do. He doesn't willingly grieve us or allow us to suffer. It is stated in Lamentations 3:

The Lord's lovingkindnesses indeed never cease, for His compassions never fail. They are new every morning; great is Thy faithfulness. (vv. 22–23, NASB)

For if He causes grief, then He will have compassion according to His abundant lovingkindness. For He does not afflict willingly, or grieve the sons of men. (vv. 32–33, KJV)

Because of this truth, I can submit to him, and in that very submission, there is great peace.

Understanding Forgiveness

Whether our conflict is with God, with others, or with our own failures, one of the difficulties many of us have with forgiveness lies in our misunderstanding of what it really means. Charles Stanley defines forgiveness as "the act of setting someone free from an obligation to you that is a result of a wrong done against you."[2] That means we are supposed to hand the issue over to God and allow him to deal with it. In the process, we confront the emotional residue left in our hearts through prayer and through continuously releasing our reactions to God.

If you're going to bury the hatchet,
bury it with the handle down. —Old saying

That sounds simple enough, but still we fight it. That is because many of our ideas about forgiveness are rooted in false assumptions. The most common of these misconceptions lies in the phrase, "Forgive and forget." In reality, there is no reason to assume that we are likely to forget what has been done to us, whether we forgive it or not. Nor should we forget—it might be dangerous for us to forget. Forgetting could set us up for a repeat performance by an unrepentant perpetrator. Forgetting can also cause us to lose sight of the negative part we may have played in the incident. In short, if we forget, we do not learn from the past.

What we do need to forget is to carry the emotional baggage our hurts have caused. With God's help, as we pray for our enemies and seek his best for them, we will be relieved of the rage, bitterness, and shame that our past hurts have brought to us. The sooner we can "forget" to feel those things, the better.

Just as forgiveness is not forgetting, neither does forgiveness mean that we trust the person who hurt us. Some people should not be trusted. Trust is earned, not demanded, and we need to develop good judgment about the trustworthiness of friends, family, and acquaintances. For example, if a family member has molested your child, has repented, and you have forgiven him, that does not mean that you should leave your child alone in his care. That would be absurd. It simply means that you have released him from his past sin. It is foolish, and perhaps even dangerous, to trust an untrustworthy person.

Forgiveness is not trust, nor is it approval of wrong behavior. We don't compromise our moral sense when we forgive—we forgive the sin against us, and in the very process, we acknowledge that it was wrong. Otherwise, there would be nothing to forgive. We don't say, "It's okay." Instead, we say, "It's *not* okay, but I'm releasing it anyway, and the consequences belong to God."

Some people who are struggling with forgiveness have a particular difficulty with the idea that they are required to reconcile with the person who wronged them. They are hindered by uncomfortable feelings, by mistrust, and perhaps even by fear for their lives. In reality, forgiveness is a requirement, while reconciliation may not necessarily be a good idea in all cases.

There are circumstances where we would be foolish to rebuild a relationship with an evil or destructive individual. And there are times when, even though we would seek reconciliation, we cannot achieve it because of the other person's unwillingness. It does take two willing persons. Forgiveness neither guarantees nor requires reconciliation.

Forgiveness does not mean, "It didn't matter."
Forgiveness does not mean, "I'll get over it in time."
Forgiveness does not mean, "There will be no penalty."
—Charles Stanley[3]

Questions about Forgiveness

Whoever you are and whatever you may think about the possibility of preventing homosexuality through loving support, gender reinforcement, and godly counsel, you have a desire for peace of mind. And that has a great deal to do with forgiveness. Once again, guilt, bitterness, and unresolved anger will block our way to peace of mind. Right now, you may be wondering:

- Is there any hope for me, when I am guilty of _____ _____?
- Is it possible to have true inner peace after I've _____ _____?
- After what _____ did to me when he/she _____, am I really expected to forgive?
- Can I ever really be free from my past experiences, when _____?
- Can my hurts from _____ be healed?

- Can my failure to help _____ever stop haunting me?
- After sinning so badly by _____, can God ever forgive me?

In my experience, that last question is the one asked most frequently by hurting people. And there's another question I always ask in response, whether I know what the person has "done wrong" or not. I ask, *"Is what you've done worse than having sex with another man's wife, and then committing premeditated murder against her husband?"* So far no one has claimed to do worse than that.

We have testimony of God's response to those very sins, dealing with David, the ancient Hebrew king. Interestingly, despite his rather appalling history, God refers to "David . . . a man after My heart, who will do all My will. For David . . . served the purpose of God in his own generation" (Acts 13:22, 36, NASB).

How did God deal with David's sin? God forgave and restored David after he repented, though he allowed him to face consequences for his actions that were very heavy to bear. David was restored and powerfully used in spite of what he had done. Jesus, in fact, was born through David's family and came through Solomon, Bathsheba's second son, the very woman with whom David had committed adultery (Matthew 1:6).

Of course, to receive God's forgiveness, David had to seek it. Fortunately, we still have the actual text of his prayer for pardon, which is recorded in Psalm 51 (NASB). David begins:

For I know my transgressions,
And my sin is ever before me.

213

Against Thee, Thee only, I have sinned,
And done what is evil in Thy sight,
So that Thou art justified when Thou dost speak,
And blameless when Thou dost judge.

*Is the church truly a community of acceptance and healing,
a community of forgiven and forgiving people? In practice,
disclosure of homosexuality has all too often led to negative
and hostile reactions even if the person in question is a non-
practicing homosexual . . . the church as a whole needs
help in reassessing its attitudes.* —Elizabeth Moberly[4]

The Quest for Peace of Mind

God is ready, willing, and able to forgive the worst sins imaginable. He can cope with any sin you or I may have committed
and wants to help us deal with the past. God calls upon us to
accept his forgiveness instead of refusing to release our guilt,
trying to punish ourselves for the past, or living in constant fear
of punishment. "If we confess our sins, he is faithful and just
and will forgive us our sins and purify us from all unrighteousness" (1 John 1:9). This means that the work has been done for
us, it is complete, and it is up to us simply to receive it.

Sin causes enormous pain. And the sin that has hurt you
the most may not have been your fault. Perhaps someone
else drastically wronged you. Are you the sinner or the
sinned against? Victim or victimizer? If you're like most of us,
in the course of a lifetime, both have been true. With that in
mind, can you identify with any of these statements?

- My father or mother ruined my life through domination
  and control.

- I have been sexually, verbally, or physically abused.

- I am an addict to sex, pornography, alcohol, or drugs.

- I am a pedophile.

- I am a sexual, verbal, or physical abuser.

- I neglected or refused to affirm my children.

- My son or daughter has become a homosexual.

- I have been involved in an adulterous relationship.

- Christians have rejected me because of my appearance and/or behavior.

- I am involved in the homosexual lifestyle.

If any of those statements apply to you, you probably have some forgiveness issues to consider. I hope you've taken to heart some of the important principles in God's Word, which I have tried to summarize in this chapter. As you forgive, you clear the way for real peace in your heart—the peace that is promised to all who trust in God. Let's remind ourselves of some of Jesus' most wonderful words:

> "Come to Me, all who are weary and heavy-laden, and I will give you rest. Take My yoke upon you, and learn from Me, for I am gentle and humble in heart; and you shall find rest for your souls. For My yoke is easy, and My load is light." (Matthew 11:28–30, NASB)
>
> "Peace I leave with you; My peace I give to you; not as the world gives, do I give to you. Let not your heart be troubled, nor let it be fearful." (John 14:27, NASB)
>
> "These things I have spoken to you, that in Me you may

have peace. In the world you have tribulation, but take courage; I have overcome the world." (John 16:33, NASB)

In the apostle Paul's letters to the churches, the Spirit of God has even more to say about peace of mind.

Therefore having been justified by faith, we have peace with God through our Lord Jesus Christ. (Romans 5:1, NASB)

And the peace of God, which surpasses all comprehension, shall guard your hearts and your minds in Christ Jesus. (Philippians 4:7, NASB)

And let the peace of Christ rule in your hearts, to which indeed you were called in one body; and be thankful. (Colossians 3:15, NASB)

Now may the Lord of peace Himself continually grant you peace in every circumstance. (2 Thessalonians 3:16, NASB)

When we receive forgiveness and cleansing through Jesus Christ (1 John 1:9), we are entitled to peace with God, peace with others, and peace with ourselves. Because we are given the tools for forgiving others and the mandate to do so, we also are released from the inner turmoil caused by anger, bitterness, and spite. Peace is our heritage as God's children. Peace is one of the fruits that our lives bear when God's Spirit dwells within us. And Jesus Christ, the Prince of Peace, wants to rule over our hearts and minds.

Will you let him?

"If my people, who are called by my name, will humble themselves and pray and seek my face and turn from their wicked ways, then will I hear from heaven and will forgive their sin and will heal their land." (2 Chronicles 7:14)

Appendix A

Questions Teenagers Ask

Q. How do I know if I'm "gay"?

A. You aren't. There is no reliable evidence that anyone is born "gay." And the Bible tells us that God doesn't want people to take part in homosexual behavior. Obviously, he wouldn't say that something is wrong, and then create people who could only function that way.

You may be asking this question because you are attracted to homosexual behavior. And you may be attracted because of things that have happened to you. You may believe you are "gay" because you have been emotionally attached to someone of the same sex, or even because you have participated in a sexual act with a person of the same sex. Perhaps you were sexually molested as a child, and because of the complicated feelings involved, you assume you are homosexual. You may think you're homosexual because people have told you that you are, or because other kids taunt you by calling you "gay," "faggot," or "dyke."

None of this indicates that you are a homosexual. Why? Because homosexual behavior is a choice people make. You may, however, have some unanswered question regarding your true, God-given gender. If so, you should talk to a trust-worthy adult.

Q. Isn't homosexuality just another alternative lifestyle?

A. Yes, homosexuality is an alternative. But it isn't "just another" one. The homosexual lifestyle is full of dangers. Most homosexuals are very promiscuous, and sexually transmitted diseases, most notably AIDS, are rampant among them. Violence is also common among homosexual partners, including higher murder rates in the gay-lesbian community. Emotional problems are widespread: depression due to loneliness and a sense of rejection contributes to a far higher suicide rate among homosexuals. Jealousies are intense, and fear and anxiety are exaggerated by the complications of same-sex relationships. Many homosexuals feel separated from God by their chosen behavior, and they are trapped by the lie that they were "born that way" or that their sins are "unforgivable." Homosexuality may be an alternative lifestyle, but it is not a good one.

Q. Can homosexuals change?

A. The answer is yes, although change isn't always easy. The longer people are involved in homosexual behavior, and the more convinced they are that they "were born this way," the more difficult change becomes. The most successful changes take place among those who deeply desire to live a normal, "straight" lifestyle, to marry and have a family. It's important to know that thousands of men and women have left their homosexual behavior behind, with God's help. Four elements for change are necessary: determination, wise counseling, accountability to a loving group of friends, and a strong relationship with God.

Q. Did Jesus say homosexual behavior is wrong?

A. Jesus clearly affirmed marriage between males and females in Matthew 19:4–5. *"Haven't you read," he replied, "that at the beginning the Creator 'made them male and female,' and said, 'For this reason a man will leave his father and mother and be united to his wife, and the two will become one flesh'? So they are no longer two, but one. Therefore what God has joined together, let man not separate."*

Specifically, the Gospels don't quote Jesus saying anything at all about homosexuality. However, in both the Old and New Testaments, homosexual behavior is described as being unacceptable to God. There are many issues that Jesus did not directly address, but we have clear direction from the Bible about them. You might want to read Leviticus 18:22 and 20:13 and Romans 1. Of course, we have to remember that the Bible speaks against many different sins and always shows that God forgives those who repent.

Q. There's a gay kid at my school and I don't want to be seen with him because people will think I'm gay too. What am I supposed to do?

A. First of all, just because everybody calls a kid "gay" doesn't mean it's true. And even if an adolescent identifies himself or herself as "gay," he or she probably hasn't participated in a same-sex relationship. These are traps vulnerable kids fall into, and by not being friendly to these kinds of boys and girls, you may unintentionally increase the likelihood that they will eventually get involved in homosexual behavior.

There are always social outcasts in groups, but Christians are specifically called to be loving and caring people. Many times it is social unacceptability that drives young people into homosexual relationships, because they feel so lost and alone. Once you understand that people aren't born "gay," you shouldn't feel so threatened by the bad choices they make or by some hidden fear that you might have been born "gay" yourself. You weren't—neither were they.

Q. Isn't saying homosexuality is wrong the same as being "homophobic"?

A. There is an important principle in dealing with people: Love the sinner and hate the sin. People who are abnormally fearful of homosexuals do not love the people involved. They mock them, shun them, and sometimes even act violently against them. This is sometimes called "homophobia," and it is just as sinful as homosexuality.

Christian love is supposed to be demonstrated to all people at all times. It doesn't mean we condone their behavior. It doesn't mean we participate in their actions or pretend they are right. It does mean that we are kind to them, and that we try to show them that God loves them, and that he wants them to live normal, healthy lives.

Q. If I'm nice to somebody who thinks he's gay, will he put a move on me? What do I do if he does?

A. Look at it this way—don't you treat a friend of the opposite sex differently if you think it is someone you might like to go out with? Most kids recognize the difference between friendship and flirting. Just being nice to someone probably won't cause him or her to think you are interested in a romantic or sexual relationship.

However, if you do find that someone has formed a same-sex emotional attachment to you, don't panic! It doesn't mean that you are "gay" or "bi" or anything else. It simply means that you should let him or her know that you aren't comfortable with the attachment and that you want to be friends, but nothing more. Sometimes that even happens with people of the opposite sex—we have to let them know we aren't interested in a relationship, even if they are. It may hurt them a little at the time, but it prevents bigger hurts later on.

If a same-sex encounter like this occurs, it is important for you to let a trustworthy adult know about the situation. That way, help can be provided for the other person as soon as possible.

Q. At my school, we were shown a video about homosexuality that made it look pretty normal and healthy. How am I supposed to respond to something like that?

A. It's true that there are some pretty outspoken pro-homosexual educational materials circulating in the public schools. Some schools are also passing out condoms to students, along with printed materials that say it's okay to have sex of any kind as long as you are protected. Because Christians and members of other religions believe God has made specific purposes for and rules about sexual behavior, they hold a more conservative moral position than people who have no faith. If the schools, which are required by law to be completely secular, offer moral alternatives that disagree with your faith, it doesn't mean you have to believe them or follow them.

Appendix B

For Further Reading

Allender and Longman. *Bold Love.* Colorado Springs: NavPress, 1992.
  Chapters include: Know the Difference Between Loving an Evil Person, a Fool and a Normal Sinner; What It Means to "Honor" a Wicked Parent; Why Anger Usually Outlives Forgiveness; How to Love an Abusive Person Without Opening Yourself up to More Damage.

Arterburn, Steve, and Jim Burns. *Drug-Proof Your Kids.* Colorado Springs: Focus, 1989.

Cloud, Henry, and John Townsend. *The Mom-Factor.* Grand Rapids: Zondervan, 1996.

Dallas, Joe. *A Strong Delusion: Confronting the "Gay Christian" Movement.* Eugene, Ore.: Harvest House, 1996.

Davies, Lori, and R. Rentzeld. *Coming Out of Homosexuality.* Downers Grove, Ill.: InterVarsity Press, 1996.

Dobson, James. *Love Must Be Tough.* Dallas: Word Publishing, 1983.

Harvey, John F. O.S. F.S. *The Truth About Homosexuality: The Cry of the Faithful.* San Francisco: Ignatius, 1996.

LaHaye, Tim, and Phillips. *Anger Is a Choice.* Grand Rapids: Zondervan, 1982.

Lewis, C. S. *Mere Christianity.* Macmillan: New York, 1986.

Mawyer, Martin. *Silent Shame.* Westchester, Ill.: Crossway Books, 1987.
The Alarming Rise of Child Sexual Abuse and How to Protect Your Children from It

Nicolosi, Joseph. *Reparative Therapy of Male Homosexuality.* Norvale, N.J.: Jason Aronson, 1991.

Olson, Joe. *When Passions Are Confused: Understanding Homosexuality* (Booklet). Grand Rapids: Radio Bible Class Ministries.
This booklet may be suitable for some young people, but should first be reviewed by leadership.

Rekers, George A. *Handbook of Child and Adolescent Sexual Problems.* New York: Lexington Books, 1995.

Rentzel, Lori. *Emotional Dependency* (Booklet). Downers Grove, Ill.: InterVarsity Press, 1990.

Satinover, Jeffrey, M.D. *Homosexuality and the Politics of Truth.* Grand Rapids: Baker Books, 1996.

Schmidt, Thomas E. *Straight & Narrow? Compassion & Clarity in the Homosexuality Debate.* Downers Grove Ill.: InterVarsity Press, 1995.

Snider, Ron. *Genuine Christianity.* Grand Rapids: Zondervan, 1996.

Socarides, Charles W., M.D. *Homosexuality: A Freedom Too Far.* Phoenix: Adam Margrave Books, 1995.

Stewart, V. Mary. *Sexual Freedom* (Booklet). Downers Grove, Ill.: InterVarsity Press, 1974.

Stott, John. *Basic Christianity.* Downers Grove: InterVarsity Press, 1971.

Wilson, Bill. *Whose Child Is This?* Lake Mary, Florida: Creation House, 1992.

Wooding, Dan. *He Intends Victory.* Irvine, CA: Promise Publishing, 1994

Worthen and Davies. *Someone I Love Is Gay.* Downers Grove: InterVarsity Press, 1996.

Yancey, Philip. *Disappointment with God.* Grand Rapids: Zondervan, 1988.

Notes

Chapter 1

1. Gershen Kaufman, *Coming Out of Shame: Transforming Gay and Lesbian Lives* (New York: Doubleday, 1996), p. 87.

2. See Andrew Sullivan, *Virtually Normal* (New York: Alfred A. Knopf, 1995), p. 199.

3. See George Rekers, Ph.D., *The Formation of a Homosexual Orientation* (New York: Lexington Books, 1995), p. 21.

4. George A. Rekers, *Handbook of Child and Adolescent Sexual Problems* (New York: Lexington Books, 1995), pp. 303–304.

5. See John Douglas, *Journey into Darkness* (New York: Scribner, 1997), pp. 363, 370–371.

6. William Stekel, M.D., *Bi-sexual Love* (Brooklyn, N.Y.: Physicians and Surgeons Book Co., 1933), p. 30.

7. Jeffrey Satinover, *Homosexuality and the Politics of Truth* (Grand Rapids: Hamewith Books, 1996), pp. 32–34.

8. See Elizabeth R. Moberly, *Homosexuality: A New Christian Ethic* (Greenwood: Attic Press, 1982); George Rekers, "Sexual Problems," in *Handbook of Treatment of Mental Disorders in Childhood and Adolescence*, ed. B. B. Wolman (Englewood Cliffs, N.J.: Prentice-Hall, 1978), pp. 268–296.

Notes

Chapter 2

1. Ellen Farmer and Deborah Abbott, *From Wedded Wife to Lesbian Life: Stories of Transformation* (1995), p. 147.
2. Quoted in Thomas E. Schmidt, *Straight & Narrow?* (Downers Grove, Ill.: InterVarsity Press, 1995), p. 49.
3. See David Wilkerson, "Homosexuality Begins at Home," in *The Marriage Affair*, ed. J. Allan Petersen (Wheaton, Ill.: Tyndale House, 1977), pp. 253–259.
4. James Dobson, *Ask Dr. Dobson* (Colorado Springs: Focus On the Family, 1998).
5. See Peter and Barbara Wyden, *Growing Up Straight* (New York: Signet, 1968) specifically Chapter 3, "How Mothers Raise Homosexual Sons"; Chapter 4, "How Fathers Raise Homosexual Sons"; Chapter 5, "How Parents Raise Homosexual Daughters"; and Chapter 6, "How the Atmosphere in the Home Can Encourage Homosexuality."
6. Jim Burns, *The Youth Builder* (Eugene, Ore.: Harvest House, 1988), pp. 273–274.
7. Lela Gilbert, personal writings.

Chapter 3

1. See Chandler Burr, *A Separate Creation: The Search for the Biological Origins of Sexual Orientation* (New York: Hyperion, 1996), p. 47.
2. John F. Harvey, O.S. F.S., *The Truth About Homosexuality* (San Francisco: Ignatius, 1995), p. 50.
3. We have provided only rough sketches of these studies. If you are interested in further details, several books provide a more thorough analysis. John F. Harvey, O.S. F.S., *The Truth About Homosexuality* (San Francisco: Ignatius, 1995) is one; also look at Thomas E. Schmidt, *Straight & Narrow?* (Downers Grove, Ill.: InterVarsity Press, 1995); and Jeffrey Satinover, *Homosexuality and the Politics of Truth* (Grand Rapids: Baker Books, 1996).
4. Thomas E. Schmidt, *Straight & Narrow?* (Downers Grove, Ill.: InterVarsity Press, 1995), p. 137.

5. David Link, "Gay Culture, Gay Identity," in *Beyond Queer* (New York: Free Press, 1996), p. 148; also see Andrew Sullivan, "Gays and the Right," pp. 65–69.

6. See Harvey, *Truth About Homosexuality*, p. 47.

7. "Fluid Sexuality," *The Advocate,* 11 July 1997, p. 6.

8. See Satinover, *Homosexuality*, p. 94.

9. Dr. Judith A. Reisman and Edward W. Eichel, *Kinsey, Sex and Fraud, The Indoctrination of a People* (Lafayette, La.: Huntington House, 1990). Also see James H. Jones, "Annals of Sexology: Dr. Yes," *The New Yorker,* 25 August–1 September 1997, pp. 98–113.

10. "The percentage of homosexuals in all societies seems to be the same and remains stable over time. Everywhere in the world, homosexual populations appear to comprise no more than 5 percent of the total population." Burr, *A Separate Creation*, p. 118.

11. Ashley MacIsaac, "Sex and Violins," *The Advocate*, 10 December 1996.

12. Judith Halberstam and Ira Livingston, eds., "Posthuman Bodies," *The Advocate*, July 1997, pp. 135–147.

13. Charles Socarides, "Exploding the Myth of Constitutional Homosexuality," *NARTH Bulletin*, September 1995, pp. 17–18.

14. Schmidt, *Straight & Narrow?*, p. 172.

Chapter 4

1. Joe Dallas, *A Strong Delusion: Confronting the "Gay Christian" Movement* (Eugene, Ore: Harvest House, 1996).

2. Peter J. Gomes, *The Good Book* (New York: William Morrow & Co., 1996), p. 158.

3. St. James Episcopal Church, November 15, 1997. Both Joe Dallas and Dawn Vukich told several such stories. One involved a lesbian suicide, which occurred after repeated attempts to find friends in a Christian youth group. Another story was of a male, struggling with homosexual feelings, who shot himself in the genitals after being told, "You can only be a part of this church after you've proved to me that you've made a decision to turn from your homosexual desires once and for all."

4. Matt. 19:14.

5. Luke 7:39–50.

Chapter 5

1. Bud Searcy, "Teens and Homosexuality: A Critical Time for Intervention," The Best of Exodus, Adolescent Issues #ADOL-001. New Creation Ministries, Fresno, CA.

2. G. Herdt and A. Boxer, *Children of Horizons* (Beacon Press: Boston, 1993).

3. Marshall Kirk and Hunter Madsen, *After the Ball: How America Will Conquer Its Fear and Hatred of Gays in the '90s* (New York: Plume, 1989), p. 259.

4. P. Rosenberger, "Psychopathology in HIV Infection: Lifetime of a Current Assessment," *Comprehensive Psychiatry Journal* 34 (1993): pp. 153–154.

5. C. S. Lewis, "Drinking Patterns in Homosexual and Heterosexual Women," *Journal of Clinical Psychiatry* 43 (1982): pp. 277–279.

6. "Health Care Needs of Gay Men and Lesbians," *Journal of the American Medical Association* 275, no. 17 (1 May 1996): p. 1357.

7. "Facts from PFLAG," quoted in *The Book: The Parent Handbook for What Matters* (San Ramon: CASA, 1997), p. 46.

8. Ibid.

9. Gabriel Rotello, *Sexual Ecology, AIDS and the Destiny of Gay Men* (New York: Dutton, 1997), p. 286.

10. "HIV/AIDS Surveillance Report," U.S. Department of Health and Human Services, Centers for Disease Control and Prevention, Year-end edition, 1995, vol. 7, no. 2, p. 10.

11. Matthew Frawley, "An Appeal to General Revelation in the Homosexuality Debate," *Princeton Theological Review* (October 1996): p. 16.

12. Sheryl Gay Stolbert, "Promiscuity and AIDS: Gays Argue Coexistence," *New York Times*, 23 November 1997.

13. Ibid.

14. Gabriel Rotello, *The Advocate*, 10 February 1996.

15. "Health Care Needs of Gay Men and Lesbians" *Journal of the American Medical Associatian*, 1 May 1996, vol. 275, #17, pp. 1355–6.

16. A. Silvestre, "Changes in HIV Rates and Sexual Behavior Among Homosexual Men 1984–1992," *American Journal of Public Health* 83 (1993): pp. 578–580.

17. Ibid.

18. Interview with author, October 1997.

19. Luke 15:17, 20–31.

Chapter 6

1. Dr. Christl R. Vonholdt, ed., *Striving for Gender Identity: Homosexuality and Christian Counseling* (Reichelsheim: German Institute for Youth and Society, 1996), p. 118.

2. Elizabeth R. Moberly, "New Perspectives on Homosexuality," *Journal of the Royal Society of Health* (December 1985): p. 206.

3. Jay Kesler, *Being Holy, Being Human* (Waco: Word, 1988), pp. 80–81.

4. Peter and Barbara Wyden, *Growing Up Straight* (New York: Signet Books, 1969), p. 50.

5. Elizabeth R. Moberly, *Homosexuality: A New Christian Ethic* (Cambridge: James Clarke & Co., 1983), p. 2.

6. Ram Dass, "Life Beyond Labels," in *Gay Soul: Finding the Heart of Gay Spirit and Nature* (San Francisco: Harper, 1994), p. 157.

Chapter 7

1. Quoted in Peterson, *Marriage Affair* (Wheaton, Ill.: Tyndale House, 1971), p. 258.

2. Peter and Barbara Wyden, *Growing Up Straight* (New York: Signet Books, 1969), p. 39

3. George Rekers, Ph.D., *Journal of Human Sexuality*, in the article

"Gender Identity Disorder" (Carrollton, TX: Lewis and Stanely, 1996), p. 14.

4. Ibid.

5. Dr. Christl R. Vonholdt, ed., *Striving for Gender Identity: Homosexuality and Christian Counseling* (Reichelsheim: German Institute for Youth and Society, 1996), p. 91.

6. Irving Bieber, *Homosexuality, a Psychoanalytic Study* (New York: Society of Medical Psychoanalysts, 1962), p. 172.

7. Oswald Chambers, *Daily Thoughts for Disciples* (Grand Rapids: Discovery House, 1994), January 10.

Chapter 8

1. Gerard Van Den Aardweg, *The Battle for Normality* (San Francisco: Ignatius Press, 1997), pp. 41–42.

2. Paul Fishbein, "Adult Video News,"*Culture Watch*, January 1998, p. 1.

3. See Brandon Taylor, *Avant-Garde and After: Rethinking Art Now* (London: Harry N. Abrams, Inc., 1995), pp. 143–165.

4. Terry Teachout, *Wall Street Journal*, 27 March 1998.

5. Marshall Kirk and Hunter Madsen, *After the Ball: How America Will Conquer Its Fear and Hatred of Gays in the '90s* (New York: Doubleday, 1989), p. 179.

6. Joseph Nicolosi, Ph.D., *Reparative Therapy of Male Homosexuality, A New Clinical Approach* (Northvale, N.J.: Jason Aronson, Inc., 1991), pp. 82–3.

7. George A. Rekers, *Handbook of Child and Adolescent Sexual Problems* (New York: Lexington Books, 1995), pp. 303–304.

8. George Barna, *Generation Next* (Ventura: Regal Books, 1995), pp. 31, 48.

9. Jerry Arterburn, *How Will I Tell My Mother?* (Nashville: Thomas Nelson, 1988), p. 72.

10. Rekers, pp. 101–131.

11. Oswald Chambers, *My Utmost for His Highest* (New York: Dodd, Mead & Co, 1935), p. 24.

12. Tony Evans, *America's Only Hope* (Chicago: Moody Press, 1990), p. 37–43.

13. Bruce Bawer, *A Place at the Table: The Gay Individual in American Society* (New York: Poseidon Press, 1993), p. 127.

14. Kirk/Madsen, *After the Ball*, p. 178.

15. Dr. Elizabeth R. Moberly, "First Aid in Pastoral Care," *The Expository Times*, June 1985, p. 265.

Chapter 9

1. Charles Stanley, *Experiencing Forgiveness* (Nashville: Thomas Nelson, 1996), pp. 56–7.

2. Ibid., p. viii.

3. Ibid., p. viii.

4. Dr. Elizabeth R. Moberly, "First Aid in Pastoral Care," *The Expository Times*, June 1985, p. 264.

Healing Wounds of the Past

Finding Inner Peace at Last

by Don Schmierer with Lela Gilbert

Don Schmierer's latest writing is a highly readable book, addressing personal pain and its consequences. He says, "I have seen so many good people—people with great potential—trapped, hindered and embittered by hurts and wounds. Some wounds are the result of domestic violence and its verbal, physical or sexual abuse; others of racial injustice or slander. Still others have come through natural disasters or the unwitting brutality of a fallen society. The intent of this book is to offer personal healing and inner peace to those who find themselves faced with some of life's most difficult circumstances."

◆————————————◆

"The simple and profound advice in Don Schmierer's book will help you recognize, reconcile and resolve critical issues which must be addressed for you to become all that He desires you to be."

Ken Canfield, Ph.D., President
National Center for Fathering

What's A Father To Do?

Facing Parents' Toughest Questions
by Don Schmierer with Lela Gilbert

This concise and readable booklet speaks directly to dads about the problems that can arise with growing kids—problems like addictions, eating disorders, promiscuity, and same-sex attractions. One father writes, "I read with great interest your small booklet What's a Father to Do? Our second son had some traits that resembled 'Sean's.' You offered excellent advice in the booklet, which I followed. I must tell you that I experienced immediate results."

◆———————————◆

"Don Schmierer provides insightful and practical advice for parents struggling to build a positive home for their children. *What's a Father to Do* provides hope for those of us seeking to reconnect families across the nation."

Ken Canfield, Ph.D., President
National Center for Fathering